Femininity, Desire and Sublimation in Psychoanalysis

Femininity, Desire and Sublimation in Psychoanalysis explores female subjectivity and examines the complexities inherent in psychoanalytic work realized by women analysts with women.

The book includes a critical study of psychoanalytic theories on femininity as well as a reflection on social aspects of gender. Elda Abrevaya envisages different paths to femininity, illustrated in the text with studies of Virginia Woolf and Marguerite Duras, and examines the vicissitudes of the relation of the little girl with the mother, and her crucial challenge, which is separation from the mother, in order to access erotic life and the use of cultural objects. *Femininity, Desire and Sublimation in Psychoanalysis* also explores the question of sublimation, shedding light on a field that has not been sufficiently explored in terms of female sexuality and female identity. Throughout the book, sublimation in women comes to the forefront as a source of satisfaction, liberation and participation in public life.

The book will be important reading for psychoanalysts and other clinicians in the field of mental health as well as academics in the fields of gender studies, literature, philosophy and sociology.

Elda Abrevaya is a founding member and a training analyst of the Istanbul Psychoanalytical Association and member of the Paris Psychoanalytic Society. She has been Professor at the University of Puerto Rico and is co-editor of the book *Homosexualities: Psychogenesis, Polymorphism, and Countertransference* (Routledge, 2015).

Psychoanalytic Ideas and Applications Series
IPA Publications Committee

Gabriela Legorreta (Montreal), Chair and Series Editor; Dominique Scarfone (Montreal); Catalina Bronstein (London); Lawrence Brown (Boston); Michele Ain (Montevideo); Carlos Moguillanski (Buenos Aires); Udo Hock (Berlin); Christine Kirchhoff (Berlin), Gennaro Saragnano (Rome) Consultant; Rhoda Bawdekar (London), Ex-officio as IPA Publishing Manager; Paul Crake (London), Ex-officio as IPA Executive Director

Recent titles in the Series include

The Infantile in Psychoanalytic Practice Today
Florence Guignard

Affect, Representation and Language
Between the Silence and the Cry
Howard B. Levine

Psychosomatics Today
A Psychoanalytic Perspective
2nd Edition
Marilia Aisenstein and Elsa Rappoport de Aisemberg

Femininity, Desire and Sublimation in Psychoanalysis
From the Melancholic to the Erotic
Elda Abrevaya

What Nazism Did to Psychoanalysis
Laurence Kahn

The Deconstruction of Narcissism and the Function of the Object
Explorations in Psychoanalysis
René Roussillon

Femininity, Desire and Sublimation in Psychoanalysis

From the Melancholic to the Erotic

Elda Abrevaya

Routledge
Taylor & Francis Group

LONDON AND NEW YORK

Cover image: Getty

First published 2023
by Routledge
4 Park Square, Milton Park, Abingdon, Oxon OX14 4RN

and by Routledge
605 Third Avenue, New York, NY 10158

Routledge is an imprint of the Taylor & Francis Group, an informa business

British Library Cataloguing-in-Publication Data
A catalogue record for this book is available from the British Library

Library of Congress Cataloging-in-Publication Data
A catalog record has been requested for this book

ISBN: 978-1-032-14080-3 (hbk)
ISBN: 978-1-032-14081-0 (pbk)
ISBN: 978-1-003-23226-1 (ebk)

DOI: 10.4324/9781003232261

Typeset in Palatino LT Std
by KnowledgeWorks Global Ltd.

To Sarah, my daughter, and to the memory
of Sara Abrevaya, my mother

Contents

Preface

In this work, we have examined some important issues with respect to female subjectivity and female sexuality, among which can be identified two principal questions: "How does one become a woman?" and "What does a woman want?" The possible answers to them are underlain by the dimension of the *feminine*. During the girl's sexual development a complex change has to take place to assure the passage from the masculine position to the feminine position. A long road has to be taken in order to resolve conflicts that originate in the early relation with the mother and they have to be examined in the light of the early oedipal phases. The little girl has to be able to "transfer" her passionate love from the mother to the father and this passage requires the imperative of separation from the maternal object. The father represents the possibility of access to the erotic object as well as to the symbolic and cultural objects, hence to sublimation.

On the road to the highly complex construction of the feminine, we understand that each woman's itinerary is unique and singular. It is in the context of the possibility of different itineraries and choices that sublimation acquires its value. The sense of accomplishment, the freedom and the *jouissance* experienced by women who can develop themselves professionally and intellectually or by those who dedicate themselves to cultural and artistic creations or to social life, have not been sufficiently examined as essential aspects of female sexuality and female subjectivity. In our trajectory throughout the book, the act of thinking and writing as an *investment of the interior life* has particularly drawn our attention and this *investment* is underpinned by the feminine. Along with the creation of literary texts, philosophical and political essays, Simone de Beauvoir was guided by the passion of writing "a novel of her interior life" and produced important autobiographical works. Virginia Woolf, on her part, expressed a similar passion when she decided to dedicate herself to "life-writing" by means of her novels. She also wrote her memoirs and a diary. She considered that she was a "self-constructed" person to the extent that she had transgressed the

Victorian society's oppressive values with respect to women and had also broken with the canons of the classical novel. Also, the works of women theorists and novelists, such as Lou Andreas-Salomé, Simone de Beauvoir, Virginia Woolf, Marguerite Duras and others, illustrate the signification that the act of writing acquires for a woman. In this case, it concerns a woman who, in the position of a desiring subject, leaves her traces and marks in the world.

Series Editor's foreword

The Publications Committee of the International Psychoanalytical Association continues, with the present volume, the series "Psychoanalytic Ideas and Applications".

The aim of this series is to focus on the scientific production of significant authors whose works are outstanding contributions to the development of the psychoanalytic field and to set out relevant ideas and themes, generated during the history of psychoanalysis, that deserve to be known and discussed by present day psychoanalysts.

The relationship between psychoanalytic ideas and their applications needs to be put forward from the perspective of theory, clinical practice, and research, to maintain their validity for contemporary psychoanalysis.

The Publication's Committee's objective is to share these ideas with the psychoanalytic community and with professionals in other related disciplines, to expand their knowledge and generate a productive interchange between the text and the reader. The IPA Publications Committee is pleased to publish the book *Femininity, Desire and Sublimation in Psychoanalysis: From the Melancholic to the Erotic* by Elda Abrevaya.

Dr Abrevaya studies crucial themes related to sexuality in general and female sexuality and subjectivity in particular. While there is significant literature on this subject, Dr Abrevaya explores new facets of female sexuality. As suggested by the title of the book, Dr Abrevaya describes a path in psychic development that allows one to move from a melancholic position to an erotic one, where desire and sublimation are possible.

Inspired by the psychoanalytic cultures of France, the United States and Argentina, she elaborates on important contemporary questions. She addresses the complex topic of gender, sexuality and the feminine and arrives at the conclusion that gender is the result of the identification *by* the parent and not the inverse. Another important topic is the feminine and new conceptions of motherhood. Dr Abrevaya argues that the new techniques used by Assisted Reproductive Technology have brought up transformations in the way motherhood and parenthood are conceived; they have changed our conception of the feminine.

Dr Abrevaya is particularly interested in the process that allows women to achieve sublimation, and as a consequence, she gives significant attention to the acts of thinking and writing as an investment of the interior life which she links to the notion of the feminine. She examines some of the work of female writers who, in her view, have been able to take the position of a desiring object and leave a trace in the world.

Skilfully organized in 11 chapters, Dr Abrevaya covers a myriad of subjects related to femininity such as the loss of the object in the young homosexual, the mother, trauma and writing, the object in Lacan and Winnicott, to name a few.

One must be thankful to Dr Abrevaya for having tackled this subject in a creative and in-depth manner. I believe this volume is an important addition to the complex subject of femininity. It will without a doubt be of interest to the psychoanalytic community as well as to other scholars who are interested in this topic.

Gabriela Legorreta
Series Editor
Chair, IPA Publications Committee

1 The mother-complex

Paranoia and the mother-complex

Before making the astonishing discovery of the little girl's passionate attachment to the mother in 'Female sexuality' (1931b) and 'Femininity' (1933a), Freud had the opportunity to study the 'mother-complex' in a young woman suffering from paranoia. In his paper 'A case of paranoia running counter to the psycho-analytic theory of disease' (1915f), he was able to relate the young woman's paranoiac delusions to her strong attachment to the mother, confirming the relation that he had already established between homosexuality and paranoia since the analysis of President Schreber (1911c). In this sense, we can establish a continuity between the papers of 1915 and 1931, contrary to J. Strachey, who considers that 'Female sexuality' was born from the repercussions produced by the 'somewhat revolutionary paper' of 'Some psychical consequences of the anatomical distinction between the sexes' (1925j). In the Editor's note to 'Female sexuality', he remarks that the text of 1925 had had an impact among the psychoanalysts and this had apparently motivated Freud to write the paper on female sexuality. In spite of acknowledging the little girl's strong attachment to her mother, Strachey does not draw the consequences of such an idea in terms of femininity. Freud's focus in 'Female sexuality' is on the pre-oedipal relation of the daughter to the mother, whereas his paper of 1925 concerns her penis-envy and the relation to the father as the oedipal object. The emphasis on the girl's penis-envy here indicates that Freud has not been able to go beyond his phallocentric point of view.

The paranoiac woman had been referred to Freud by her lawyer. The latter had needed a psychiatric expertise in order to evaluate her accusation in regard to the man who had been her lover. She accused him of secretly introducing witnesses into the room with the purpose of photographing them while they were making love. The lawyer, quite experienced in his field, had a flair that her accusation was pathological. Freud had two interviews with her, demonstrating his fine clinical tact and perception of the situation. This beautiful woman of thirty years old had

DOI: 10.4324/9781003232261-1

never been involved in a love affair with a man and lived alone with her old mother since her father had died. A young man who worked in the same office with her proposed they should spend some time together. As this handsome and cultivated young man was married, they had to meet in his bachelor rooms during the day. One day while they were kissing and embracing each other, she was suddenly startled by a kind of knock or click and had asked him what the noise was about. When they had left the room, she had seen two men on the staircase, who seemed to be whispering to each other about her. She had thought that the small box that one of them was carrying was a camera and that one of the men had been hidden behind the curtain inside the room to take their photograph while they were making love. Hence, she had attributed the noise that she had heard to the camera. She had asked the young man for an explanation of what had happened. He had tried to reassure her but had not been successful in doing so.

The aspects presented with respect to the young woman seem, at first sight, to be in contradiction with Freud's theory of paranoia, developed by means of the analysis of President Schreber (1911c). Freud had established an intimate connection between male paranoia and homosexual tendencies, discovering that the father-complex resided in the centre of President Schreber's delusion of persecution. He had found out that the main proposition 'I (a man) *love him* (a man)' was contradicted by: 'I do not *love* him – I *hate* him'. 'I hate him' was transformed by the mechanism of projection: '*He hates* (persecutes) *me*, which will justify me in hating him'. Hence, due to the mechanism of projection, the internal perception appears as the consequence of an external perception. The subject hates the other man because he persecutes him. The publication of the paper on the paranoiac woman came four years later than the paper on President Schreber. Freud, in a brilliant way, found out that the analysis of the young woman's delusion of persecution did not come into contradiction with his theory of paranoia. The only difference consisted in that it was a woman's paranoia in whose centre lay the mother-complex, in opposition to the father-complex underlying the paranoia of President Schreber.

The young woman seemed to defend herself against her love for the young man and she realized it by transforming him into a persecutor and apparently there was no indication of a conflict with respect to a homosexual attachment. However, the second interview with the young woman provided the key to the understanding of her delusion, the key element being the mother. During the second interview the young woman added some details that facilitated the comprehension of the situation. The day after their first visit to the bachelor rooms, she had seen the young man in the office in a business meeting with the female director. The latter was an elderly lady, who was very fond of her. She described her to Freud as such: 'She has white hair like my mother' (1915f, p. 266). When she saw the young man and the female director speaking in low voices, she had thought that he was telling her about their love affair. Freud's emphasis here is on her fantasy of a sexual scene taking place between the elderly lady, as a mother-substitute, and the young man, put in the place of the father. This scene has the value of a primal scene. Freud made use of the concept of 'primal phantasies' that he would extensively discuss in *Introductory lectures* (1916–1917) and particularly in the case of the 'Wolf man' (1918b). Freud underlies the paranoiac character of the young woman's two delusions, independently of the circumstances that had taken place. No matter what had happened, she was inclined to perceive them in a persecutory mode. The first delusion refers to the noise that she had heard in the room and the second consists in imagining the meeting between the elderly lady and the young man as something intimately sexual, both scenes leading her to suspect the lover. However, the original persecutor was the mother.

> The *original* persecutor – the agency whose influence the patient wishes to escape – is here again not a man but a woman [...] The patient's attachment to her own sex opposed her attempts to adopt a person of the other sex as a love–object. Her love for her mother had become the spokesman of all those tendencies which, playing the part of a 'conscience', seek to arrest a girl's first step along the new road to normal sexual satisfaction – in many respects a dangerous one, and indeed it succeeded in disturbing her relationship with men. The original here is 'her relation with men'.
>
> (1915f, p. 267)

The young woman had not been able to free herself from her mother's influence and had succumbed to a paranoiac delusion, indicating 'the presence of a mother-complex which is as a rule over-powerful and is certainly unmastered' (1915f, p. 267). The mother-complex served the purpose of keeping her away from men. After having been attracted to the young man, she tried to struggle against her strong homosexual love. The accidental noise that the young woman had heard had activated the fantasy of the primal scene, which underlay the scene between her lover and the elderly lady. So, the accidental noise in the first encounter with her lover 'was thus merely playing the part of a provoking factor which activated the typical phantasy of overhearing which is a component of the parental complex' (1915f, p. 269). While the lover substituted the father, she took her mother's place – she *became* her mother, by means of identification. This position permitted her to take the father (lover) as a sexual object, liberating her from her homosexual attachment to the mother. Hence, the activation of the fantasy of the primal scene produced a change in which the identification with the mother replaced the erotic investment of the mother. The identification with her mother led the young woman to take the father (lover) as a sexual object.

The unconscious solution that she found to her conflict was realized by means of regression:

> instead of choosing her mother as a love–object, she identified herself with her – she herself *became* her mother. The possibility of this regression points to the narcissistic origin of her homosexual object–choice and thus to the paranoic disposition in her.
>
> (1915f, p. 269).

While Freud discusses the nature of the young woman's pathological reaction, he remarks that it was not determined by her actual relations to the mother but 'by her infantile relations to her earliest image of her mother' (1915f, p. 268). This idea anticipates the powerful impact that the girl's early attachment has in her psychical reality, as Freud will discover in 'Female sexuality'. In the latter, he identifies the girl's early dependence on the mother as the germ of female paranoia.

In spite of having analysed the paranoiac woman's conflicts in relation to her mother, the 'mother-complex' stays as an isolated finding in Freud's theory of sexuality till the publication of 'Female sexuality', separated almost by an interval of fifteen years. The discovery of the girl's early attachment provides the opportunity of tracing the origin of hysteria to the fixations on the mother: 'this phase of attachment to the mother is especially related to the aetiology of hysteria, which is not surprising when we reflect that both the phase and the neurosis are characteristically feminine' (1931b, p. 227). In *Inhibitions, symptoms and anxiety* (1926d), Freud had already identified that hysteria had a strong affinity with femininity. He had given a central place to the anxiety provoked by the threat of the loss of the object's love and had compared its intensity with the castration anxiety in the boy, but he had not been able to situate this problematic in the phase of the early attachment to the mother. Also, in the previous year in 'Some psychical consequences of the anatomical distinction between the sexes', Freud had defended the idea that the female super-ego could never be as strong as that in the male because castration anxiety did not operate in her psychic reality. Freud's discovery in 1926 of the major impact of the threat of losing the object is a crucial element in terms of female subjectivity. This perspective will fully find its place in Melanie Klein and Ernest Jones. In this sense, the thesis with respect to the central place occupied by the threat of the loss of the object's love is complementary to the findings with respect to the girl's early attachment.

The super-ego's impact on the girl

Melanie Klein conceived the Oedipus complex from its early phases and established a continuity between the pre-genital and the genital processes. However, a radical divergence arose between Melanie Klein and Freud with respect to the super-ego's influence in the early phases. Melanie Klein, who was working on *The psycho-analysis of children* (1932), had already written a chapter on the impact of the early anxiety situations on the girl's sexual development. She had found out that Freud had published 'Female sexuality' omitting the super-ego's influence on the girl's psyche and she strongly criticized him for having left out this question and the guilt feelings with respect to the mother. She considered that the girl's primary libidinal tie to the object is, from very early on, reinforced by anxiety and guilt emanating from her aggressive drives. The girl's hostility arises not only from the inevitable frustrations that characterize maternal care but also from her envy with regard to the mother, who possesses the penis (the father) and the babies. Melanie Klein's criticism with respect to Freud's conception of female sexuality reflects her passion in terms of a theory in the heart of which lies the antagonism between the super-ego and the libidinal drives. The impact of the super-ego on the libidinal drives can only be grasped if its formation is situated in the early oedipal phases. The Kleinian super-ego is constituted from the introjection of the good and the persecuting objects and its cruelty is proportional to the intensity of the child's sadistic drives, whereas in Freud it is a post-oedipal formation. The Freudian super-ego is the heir of the Oedipus complex and its differentiation into the ego ideal embodies collective ideals and cultural acquisitions. Or, our psychoanalytic experience indicates the strong influence of the super-ego in the girl's psychical reality, incomparably more cruel than in the boy. What creates this psychic difference is due to a basic threat, that of losing the object and its love.

If we return to the paranoiac woman, we cannot grasp her conflicts unless we include the super-ego's impact to the extent that it reactivates anxieties with respect to the earliest image of the mother. Her feelings of guilt, provoked by an erotic experience with the young man, erected an obstacle to her separation from her. The elderly lady, as a mother substitute, had been perceived as a castrating figure prohibiting having sex and enjoying it.

> Her love for her mother had become the spokesman of all those tendencies, which playing the part of a 'conscience', seek to arrest a girl's first step along the new road to normal sexual satisfaction – in many respects a dangerous one and indeed it succeeded in disturbing her relation with men.
>
> (1915f, p. 267).

Or, during adolescence the girl has to struggle to 'emancipate' herself from the mother, who tries to control and repress her sexuality. In the analysis of the mother-complex, Freud notes: 'If in the attempt to emancipate herself she falls a victim to a neurosis it implies the presence of a mother-complex which is as a rule over-powerful, and is certainly unmastered'

(1915f, p. 267). Engaged in early oedipal processes, the little girl experiences anxiety and guilt with respect to the mother because the father is already a libidinal object for her. However, in 'Female sexuality', Freud considers that the little girl's early attachment to the mother is 'exclusive' and leaves out the father both as a libidinal object and as a rival. Or, in the Kleinian conception, the girl's oedipal conflicts arise very early, in the turmoil created between her erotic drives in regard to the father and her guilt feelings with respect to the mother. These conflicts lead eventually to the necessity to renounce temporarily the feminine position and adopt the phallic position (Jones, 1927). When the fear of retaliation coming from the mother exceeds certain limits, the girl cannot detach herself from the object. In 'The early development of female sexuality' (1927), Ernest Jones speaks of *aphanisis*, which is the fear of a total and permanent abolition of the capacity to take pleasure that is provoked by the threat of losing the object's love. The girl's libidinal drives with respect to the father provoke the fear of being abandoned by the mother. Jones notes that the analysis of women allows a deeper understanding of the relation between privation of the sexual desire (*aphanisis*) and feelings of guilt. In other words, the relation between the two forces permits us to comprehend the very complex question of the super-ego. In the Kleinian theory, the inevitable frustration with respect to the breast in the oral stage leads the little girl to displace her libido to the penis, which is fantasized as being inside the mother's body. Melanie Klein, like Freud, considers that the libido is transferred from the maternal object to the paternal one, but with the difference that she situates this process in an earlier phase. The child in the Kleinian theory has already reached the capacity to imagine and fantasize the maternal body as a container of partial objects, such as the penis, babies and faeces.

Both Freud's and Melanie Klein's findings in regard to female sexuality permit us to build a theoretical edifice in whose foundation lies the girl's early attachment to the mother. The early attachment constitutes the narcissistic and homosexual basis on which the erotic relation to the father is erected. In 'Female sexuality', Freud is surprised to discover that in the second phase in which the father begins to play a role in the girl's eroticism, he has scarcely contributed 'any new feature to her erotic life' (1931b, p. 225). The second phase is merely a 'transference' from the first, as Freud argues in 'Femininity' (1933a). Thus, the woman's erotic life is rooted in the soil of her narcissistic and homosexual tie to the primary object, which determines the quality of her erotic life. In this sense, we do not share the view of James Strachey, who indicates in his 'Editor's Note' to 'Female sexuality' that the latter is a reformulation of Freud's findings already announced in 'Some psychical consequences of the anatomical distinction between the sexes' (1925j). On the contrary, we consider that there is a rupture between the two approaches. The findings on female sexuality open a reflexion in terms of depth and interiority of the female body, whereas the article of 1925 consists in a phallic point of view referring to the surface of her body. Freud had already recognized in 'A child is being beaten', the impossibility of a precise analogy between the female and the male sexual developments: 'the expectation of there being a complete parallel was mistaken' (1919e, p. 196). So, for Strachey the differentiation between male sexuality and female sexuality that Freud clearly establishes in 1925j, represents notable progress in terms of a theory of female sexuality. The girl's penis-envy creates the condition of her displacement to the father, a schema in which the role of the mother is by no means taken into consideration. Or, if we take a close look at the girl's femininity as examined in 'A child is being beaten', the paper of 1925 represents a regression from her femininity to her phallicism (1925j). The first allows us to establish a continuity between the highly erotic fantasy of being beaten by the father and the underlying incestuous fantasies. These feminine fantasies constitute essential moments of infantile sexuality with all their sensuality. However, the father as the erotic object of the girl disappears in the paper of 1925, acquiring a purely masturbatory signification (André, 1995). Also, Freud's shift in regard to female sexuality in 1931 consists in the relinquishment of the girl's phallicism to the extent that it includes a new vertex related to the mother. The girl's early attachment places in the centre of our reflexion, *the question of separation from the mother as an on-going and never ending challenge for women during their life time.*

References

André, J. (1995). *Aux origines féminines de la sexualité*. Paris: PUF.

Freud, S. (1911c). Psycho-analytic notes on an autobiographical account of a case of paranoia (dementia paranoides). *SE: 12*, 3–82.

Freud, S. (1915f). A case of paranoia running counter to the psychoanalytic theory of disease. *SE: 14*, 263–272.

Freud, S. (1918b). From the history of an infantile neurosis. *SE: 17*, 7–122.

Freud, S. (1919e). A child is being beaten. *SE: 17*, 179–204.

Freud, S. (1925j). Some psychical consequences of the anatomical distinction between the sexes. *SE: 19*, 243–258.

Freud, S. (1926d). *Inhibitions, symptoms and anxiety. SE: 20*, 77–175.

Freud, S. (1931b). Female sexuality. *SE: 21*, 223–243.

Freud, S. (1933a). Femininity. *New introductory lectures on psycho-analysis. SE: 22*, 3–182.

Jones, E. (1927). The early development of female sexuality. *International journal of psychoanalysis, 8*, 459–472.

Klein, M. (1932). *The psycho-analysis of children*. London: Hogarth.

2 Loss of the object in the young homosexual

The study of the case of the young homosexual shows us the complexity of the girl's sexual development and the obstacles that stand in the way of accessing femininity. These obstacles arise from her early attachment to the mother. The girl's subjectivity bears the marks of the torments caused by her early attachment, as well as those of her struggle to tear herself away from her mother to access to eroticism, creativity and sublimation. What is it that lies in the nature of this passion that makes separation between mother and daughter so conflicted? The clinical study of the young homosexual is of great interest not only because of her love for a woman, but also because of the complexity of her ties to the double love object, the mother and the father. The lack of stabilization of the object–choice in the young homosexual is illustrative of the girl's conflicted tie to the mother and her difficulty in detaching herself from the object. In 'The psychogenesis of a case of homosexuality', Freud does not, however, consider the oscillation between the mother and the father as a specificity of female sexuality. On the contrary, he thinks that it is valid for both sexes. 'In all of us, throughout life, the libido normally oscillates between male and female objects' (1920a, p. 158). A 'special factor' contributes finally to the election and stabilization of the object.

> Naturally, when the swing-over is fundamental and final, we suspect the presence of some special factor which definitely favours one side or the other, and which perhaps has only waited for the appropriate moment in order to turn the choice of object in its direction.
>
> (1920a, p. 158)

However, Freud remarks that bisexuality in the girl is stronger than in the boy to the extent that her relation to the double love object continues to exist.

We shall approach the young girl's case in three different times: the first corresponds to Freud's study; the second to Lacan's discussion in his seminars *La relation d'objet* (1956–1957) and *L'angoisse* (1962–1963); and the third consists of a biographical book, *Sidonie Csillag* (Rieder & Voigt, 2004).

DOI: 10.4324/9781003232261-2

Lacan remarks that this case is one of the brightest, yet one of the most disconcerting of Freud's cases and this is true. It disconcerts us because it involves a very serious attempt at suicide when there is no manifestation of neurotic symptoms or complaints with respect to psychical conflicts. By consequence, the young girl is not 'ill' and has no demand to make to Freud with regard to analysis. Also, through her biographical book, we will learn that there had been two more attempts at suicide. On the other hand, her case confronts us with complex identifications that are interwoven and are of a libidinal as well as narcissistic nature. Freud's counter-transference is the reason for a blind spot that impedes him from grasping her positive transference, as revealed through her dreams. The latter consist of the realization of an unconscious desire for a man's love as well as her wish to have children. But Freud, in a surprising way, and in contradiction with his own theory of dreams, does not believe in the sincerity of her unconscious desire, as expressed through her dreams. However, despite his prejudices he can advance in the moving sands of the conceptualization of the young girl's homosexuality that he realizes brilliantly. The difficulty in understanding the young girl's libidinal patterns and identifying them with respect to her infantile objects creates a challenging reading for us – this difficulty being particularly provoked by the oscillation between the male and female objects. Hence, the richness of the case is due to the heterogeneity of psychic time, in which the loss of the object in narcissistic terms is subject to re-organizations and re-managements and finds expression in the attempts at suicide. This case appears a year after the publication of the essay 'A child is being beaten' (1919e), in which Freud elaborates a genital fantasy, typically feminine with respect to the father. Despite that the study of the young homosexual has been realized ten years before the publication of 'Female sexuality' (1931b), it anticipates in a curious way the girl's early tie to the mother.

Time 1: Freud's encounter with the young homosexual

The young homosexual was eighteen years old when she met Freud. So, she is a young girl for us and not 'a woman', as the title in the English translation indicates. Her case bears similarities with that of Dora, who was also of the same age when she began analysis with Freud. In *La relation d'objet* (1956–1957), Lacan discusses their similarities. In both of them, it is the father who solicits the analytical treatment for the daughter and the demand for treatment is caused by a family crisis in whose centre lies a woman, who is the source of the conflict. Dora's father expected his daughter to receive treatment so that he would not be bothered in his relation with Mrs K, whereas for the young homosexual's father it was the intolerable presence of the society-lady that was the motive of his demand for his daughter's treatment. So, each time there is a desired woman in the centre of a triangle constituted by the father, the daughter and the other woman. While Mrs K is Dora's object of adoration, the society-lady is effectively the young homosexual's object of desire. Freud does not define the young homosexual as a patient and has his doubts about the father's demand, as he knows that nobody can be converted from homosexuality to heterosexuality, specially when there is a fixation on the object of the same sex. It is noteworthy to observe that Freud's scientific position with respect to homosexuality is very open and far from being moralistic, a position that he maintained in his writings on sexuality from the *Three essays* (1905d) till the end of his life. The father perceived his daughter's homosexuality as something abnormal and also as a problem that could harm his reputation. He was a very successful and well-known industrialist in Viennese society. In this sense, he was determined to try all the alternatives in order to change his daughter's sexual inclinations. He had sent his daughter to Freud but he was resolute about arranging a marriage for her in case psychoanalysis did not work. The real obstacles that lie in the conversion of homosexuality into heterosexuality and the lack of motivation for treatment were not the only factors that impeded the therapeutic transformation of the young girl. Freud's prejudices also had an impact on this analysis.

It is surprising that Freud who had given a name, a pseudonym, for his female patients, such as Emmy, Lucy, Elisabeth, Cäcilie and Katharina, had left the young homosexual without a name. He had even given a pseudonym to Katharina who he had met in the mountains while he was having a walk. Freud's designation of his young patient as 'the young homosexual' seems disturbing because the psychic problematic here coincides with a social problematic that has discriminatory implications. Freud's resistances at this point can only be understood if the analysis of the young homosexual is situated in the period of the analysis of his daughter Anna. We know that Freud had intended the impossible by analysing his daughter in two different periods. The first took place between 1918 and 1922 and the second between 1924 and 1925. In the origins of psychoanalysis it was quite usual for psychoanalysts to analyse their children. In this sense, the resistances that Freud manifested in the young homosexual's analysis were related to his difficulty in acknowledging his daughter's homosexuality (Young-Bruehl, 1991). He committed serious errors during the young girl's treatment which he ended after three months. Contrary to Dora who had interrupted her analysis after three months, it was Freud who had abandoned the young homosexual. Freud had met the young girl six months after her first attempt at suicide. In reality, it is the only one that we know about till the publication of the biographical book *Sidonie Csillag* (2004). Freud's study of the case in 1920 and Lacan's discussion of it in his seminars *La relation d'objet* (1956–1957) and *L'angoisse* (1962–1963) have, therefore, focused on the first attempt. The gravity of the first attempt can only be grasped in the light of the other two that we discover through the reading of her biography. In the period that had preceded the young girl's analysis with Freud, the parents could not understand the reason why their daughter had fallen in love with a woman ten years her elder and, worst of all, of bad reputation. All the prohibitions of the father could not impede her from meeting her beloved. One day the inevitable took place when the father met his daughter in the street, who was walking in the company of the lady. He cast a furious look at them and walked away. When the lady found out that this man was the young girl's father, she told her that their relation could not continue in this way. On hearing these words, the young girl had rushed off and thrown herself over the bridge onto the railway line. After this serious attempt, both the parents' and the lady's attitude with respect to her had become more indulgent.

Repudiation of femininity

For Freud and Lacan, the young girl's object of desire is the father and their respective studies focus on her relation to him. Freud notes that the disappointment with respect to the unconscious wish to have a child from the father had led to the repudiation of her femininity, as the mother had born the child she longed for. The force of the incestuous desire to have a child draws Lacan's attention and the young girl's desire seems to be more than something imaginary. This fantasy, experienced almost in a real way, would explain the intensity of her disappointment. Disappointments are inevitable in the Oedipus situation and stem from the realization that the incestuous wish with regard to the parent of the opposite sex does not conform to the reality-principle. Thus, the reality-principle imposes on the child of both sexes the necessity to renounce the incestuous object. The little girl cannot take the risk of losing her mother, who is the source of her life as well as the satisfaction of her vital needs. In 'Femininity' Freud remarks: 'The significance of these disappointments must not be exaggerated; a girl who is destined to become feminine is not spared them, though they do not have the same effect' (1933a, p. 130). When Freud mentions that these disappointments 'do not have the same effect', he probably had in mind the example of the young homosexual who had overreacted to the Oedipus situation. The disappointment caused by the mother who had given birth to a boy, had brought about the repudiation of her femininity. The fact that the father had been the libidinal object of the young girl is an indicator for Freud that female homosexuality is not necessarily a direct continuation of infantile masculinity. He is categorical when he notes that it is seldom a continuation of an infantile masculine complex. In this sense, we can see to what degree the assumption of femininity is complex. The girl experiences disappointments that are provoked by the discovery that the mother is the father's lover and that her tiny body is not adequate for genital satisfaction with him.

The unconscious solution to her incestual wishes that the young homosexual had found was to renounce the rivalry with the mother, and thus her femininity that she left to her. She became homosexual in order to not lose her and assure her love. In reality, she had not received femininity as a gift from her, the way mothers transmit it symbolically to their daughters, through the mirror of their gaze and words. This mirror serves to acknowledge and support their femininity. A girl needs to have confidence in the reliability and love of the maternal object in order to enter into competition with her as femininity can only be built on the existence of a firm narcissistic ground that ensues from the reliability of the object. Freud indicates the motive that underlay the young girl's renunciation of men. 'If, then, the girl became homosexual and left men to her mother (in other words, 'retired in favour of' her mother), she would remove something which had hitherto been partly responsible for her mother's dislike' (1920a, p. 158–159). Hence, the motive to be loved by the mother becomes an essential piece of Freud's theory on female sexuality, as he will formulate in *Inhibitions, symptoms and anxiety* (1926d). However, the assumption of femininity comprises risks. The little girl has to persist in her feminine desire with respect to the father, in spite of the conflicts caused by the threat of losing her mother's love. Femininity has a price for each woman, who faces the necessity of reparation of her aggressive drives with respect to the mother as well as the imperative of separation in order to experience *jouissance* with the lover. Separation implies having gone through the mourning(s) of the maternal object. The word 'mourning' in plural signifies that the girl has to surmount the conflicts specific to the stages or cycles of life, such as puberty, sexual life, maternity, menopause, ageing and so on. In each stage, her relation to her infantile objects are restructured *après-coup* (Lacan, 1977), leading to the necessity to elaborate her separation and differentiation from the object.

Regression to narcissism

The young homosexual had not been able to overcome the disappointment that she had experienced with respect to the father and had reacted from an extreme position by rejecting her femininity. She had turned away from him and men in general, had repudiated her wish for a child and had realized it through her identification with the father. Thus, she *became* the father and chose the object of the father's desire, the mother (or her substitute). In trying to explain the identification of the young homosexual with the father, Freud adds a footnote in which he underlines the narcissistic nature of the loss that takes places in some cases.

> It is by no means rare for a love-relation to be broken off through a process of identification on the part of the lover with the loved object, a process equivalent to a kind of regression to narcissism. After this

has been accomplished, it is easy in making a fresh choice of the object to direct the libido to a member of the sex opposite to that of the earlier choice.

(1920a, p. 158)

In the case of the paranoiac woman that we discussed in Chapter 1, a regression to narcissism had also taken place. The unconscious solution that she had found to her conflict between her desire for the young man and her attachment to the mother had been by means of regression. She herself had *become* her mother and had taken the father (or his substitute) as a sexual object, an act that liberated her from an erotic investment of the mother. In the case of the paranoiac woman, as well as the young homosexual, regression indicates the narcissistic origin of the fixation on the homosexual object. In the case of the young homosexual, the identification with the loved object, the father, had led to a masculine position and the libido had regressed to the mother. Here, the regression to a libidinal object differentiates this process from melancholia. We know that in melancholia a disappointment coming from the love object provokes the destruction of the object–relationship that had once existed. Hence, the subject does not know what has been lost, particularly when the loss has taken place before the development of the ego and verbal language. After having retired the libido from the lost object, the subject is incapable of displacing it with a new one. Therefore, the object can never be mourned. As Benno Rosenberg (1991) remarks, melancholia is not characterized by a never-ending mourning but by the impossibility of mourning the lost object, and that is its paradox. Comparing mourning and melancholia, Freud (1917e) distinguishes the first by pointing out that reality-testing will come to life after having hypercathected the memories related to the lost object, whereas in melancholia there is no such possibility.

The young girl's libidinal regression to the maternal object seemed enigmatic to the extent that the object had never cherished her. Freud offers a bright explanation of this object–choice, relating it to her conflict with the mother: 'her relation to her mother had certainly been ambivalent from the beginning, and it proved easy to revive her earlier love for her mother and with its help to bring about an overcompensation for her current hostility towards her' (1920a, p. 158). Freud's analysis of the young homosexual's object–choice reflects the complexity underlying the daughter's relation to the mother. Her hostile feelings were provoked by the fact that the mother had won in the competition, as she was the one who had procreated a son from her husband. The nature of the young girl's hostility in regard to the mother was twofold. It was not only oedipal but also narcissistic. We know that a girl can have a strong fixation on a mother who has been incapable of perceiving her daughter's needs. Narcissistic traumas that are produced in early childhood can be the occasion of such fixations. The longing for the mother's love had oriented the young girl's libido to female figures. As a child she had been in love with a strict school teacher, who resembled her mother. After having experienced a disappointment with respect to the father, she directed her libido to women who had children. Later she changed to those who were not mothers and then she moved to an extreme point, to women of bad reputation. She felt great compassion for the society-lady and strongly wished to save her from a debased position. The masculine position in which she situated herself is similar to that occupied by some men who can only desire women of bad reputation 'whose fidelity and reliability are open to some doubt' (Freud, 1910h, p. 166). While these men are not sexually aroused by their loyal and tender wives, they can fully enjoy the sexual act with women of 'bad reputation' by giving free rein to their perverse fantasies. In their unconscious, in fact, the mother is a prostitute who enjoys sex with the husband. So, this kind of object–choice in men derives from the incestual attachment to the mother; while in the young homosexual the masculine type of object–choice is derived from the fixation on the mother. She felt that her mother knew how to seduce her husband and other men and in this sense she was a prostitute who knew all about sex.

Lacan, like Freud, defines the young homosexual's dedication and humility with respect to the lady as being essentially masculine. The young girl offered her unconditional love to the beloved despite there being no reciprocity on the part of the lady. Her mode of love was devoid of sensuality and Freud observed that sensual satisfactions provoked revulsion in her. In fact, the disgust with regard to sensual satisfaction continued to be one of her major difficulties in her adult sexual life, as she later communicated to the authors of her biography. According to Freud, a man's dedication to the beloved is masculine, while the exigent demand to be loved characterizes female narcissism. The intensification of primary narcissism during puberty would impede the complete development of a 'true' object–choice in women, whereas object–love with its accompanying sexual overvaluation would fully develop in men. In 'On narcissism: an introduction', what seems surprising is that Freud (1914c) offers a biological explanation for the intensification of primary narcissism in the girl and attributes it to the maturation of the genital organs at the onset of puberty. The girl who grows up to become a beautiful woman, would only love herself. 'Strictly speaking, it is only themselves that such women love with an intensity comparable to that of the man's love for them. Nor does their need lie in the direction of loving, but of being loved' (1914c, p. 89). However, Freud feels the need to affirm that those differences between men and women are not universal and that there are women who can love according to 'the masculine type'. In spite of attributing the possibility for some women of being able to fully love the object, at the same time he calls it 'the masculine type'. What counts, beyond the male or female type of object–love, is the desire to be loved, which places each subject, be it a man or a woman, in a feminine position (Cournut, 2015).

The heterogeneity of time and the concept of *Nachträglichkeit*

Freud offers a bright study of the young homosexual that is not linear and he is capable of transmitting the paradoxes inherent to her relation to the infantile objects. His reading includes an analysis of the psychical processes that take place 'in different layers of the mind' (1920a, p. 160), thus suggesting the heterogeneity of time. This idea reminds us of the definition that Freud has given of the concept of *Nachträglichkeit* in the origins of psychoanalysis. In his letter to Fliess on December 6, 1896, he hypothesizes that the psychical apparatus is engendered by 'stratification' and that memory traces undergo a reorganization when new events are concerned (Masson, 1985). These 'new events' correspond to traumatic ones in sexual terms. In his seminar *L'après-coup* (2006), Jean Laplanche comments that since Freud's letter to Fliess, the theory of *après-coup* has become the general frame of a theory of the psychical apparatus. After Freud's death, which had produced the quasi-effacement of the concept in Freudian theory, Lacan (1966) was the first analyst to recuperate its specificity. Freud did not name the concept of *Nachträglichkeit* when he observed the presence of 'different layers' in the young homosexual's psyche. In 1896, he defined a stratification that referred to reorganizations of the memory traces in the light of traumatic events, thus implying the existence of different psychical times. Even if he did not name the concept of *Nachträglichkeit*, he added an important dimension to his reflexion on causality by establishing a connection between the young homosexual's disappointment that had led to her identification with the father and the libidinal regression to the mother. The latter had been the object of fixation in an earlier period of childhood. Hence, we are speaking of the existence of different times during the sexual development: her early attachment and fixation on the mother, the displacement to the father and the regression to the maternal object at the onset of puberty.

The impossibility of realizing a linear reading of this case is clear when Freud discusses the motives underlying the young girl's attempt at suicide. At a first reading, we are inclined to think that the precipitating factor for her attempt at suicide was the father's rejection of his daughter when he had met her in the company of the lady. But a few lines further on, Freud remarks that the lady, who had just discovered that the man was the father of the young girl, had ordered her to end the relation. 'In her despair at having thus lost her loved for ever, she wanted to put an end to herself' (1920a, p. 162). Thus, Freud places the weight of the attempt at suicide in the lady's rejection. His analysis is of great subtlety as he notes that the lady had, in fact, uttered the same prohibition as the father in regard to the relation. Hence, the young girl faced a double threat, the impending threat of losing both objects, the lady as a substitute of the mother and the father. On the other hand, Freud sheds light on the enigmatic question of how a person can find the force to end his or her life despite the powerful life instinct. He remarks:

> probably no one finds the mental energy required to kill himself unless, in the first place, in doing so he is at the same time killing an object with whom he has identified himself, and, in the second place, is turning against himself a death-wish which had been directed against someone else.

(1920a, p. 162)

At this point, the object that the young girl would like to kill is the mother, 'who should have died at the birth of the child denied to herself' (1920a, p. 163). We would like to underline the word 'denied', which has weight here. As Lacan remarks, in the young homosexual the wish to have a child by the father was more than a fantasy and this was a problem.

Time 2: Lacan's analysis of the young homosexual

The phallus

In his seminar *La relation d'objet* (1956–1957), Lacan examines the young homosexual's traumatic experience from the perspective of the phallus. He uses the concept of *frustration* to discuss the young girl's traumatic experience when the mother was the one who had born the child by the father. *Frustration* is part of a conceptual triad in his theory, together with *privation* and *castration*. The three of them refer to aspects of lack and incompleteness with respect to the phallus. The phallus is not the anatomical organ, the penis, nor a fantasy, but a signifier, the signifier of desire. The subject's needs have to pass through language and be transformed into a signifying form that corresponds to a demand. As the need cannot be fully articulated by means of language, it reappears as desire. The needs return to the subject in an alienated form in as much as they are subjected to the demand, that is to language. Lacan refers to a real lack in the girl as *privation*, inspired by Karen Horney's (1967) concept of the term. However, the lack of the anatomical organ has no value in itself unless we speak of the phallus. The terms *privation, frustration* and *castration* designate respectively the real, the imaginary and the symbolic instances. *Frustration* represents an imaginary damage with regard to the phallus. Lacan conceptualizes the young homosexual's traumatic experience in terms of the frustration of her wish to possess the phallus=child. However, this explanation does not seem to reflect the force of the young girl's traumatic experience in narcissistic terms. The notion of *disappointment* seems to us to designate better the force of her narcissistic injury, helping us to explain the rupture that had taken place with regard to the father. The impact of the narcissistic injury can be grasped only if we consider that it referred to an earlier disappointment with respect to the mother. However, the narcissistic injury in melancholia is much more radical and seems to have no reparation: 'An object–choice, an attachment of the libido to a particular person, had at one time existed; then owing to a real slight or disappointment coming from the loved person, the object–relationship was shattered' (Freud, 1917e, pp. 248–249).

In *La relation d'objet*, Lacan does not refer to the absence of a penis but to that of the phallus in the girl, to the extent that the first simply does not have a place in the dialectic of desire. The desire with respect to the phallus requires its being received as a gift (*don*). Once the girl realizes her lack with regard to the phallus, her libido is orientated to the father, who can offer it to her as a gift, as an expression of his virility. In other words, the phallus as a signifier is elevated to the rank of gift. At one point in the Oedipus situation, the little girl has to acknowledge that she cannot have the phallus=child from the father, according to the law regarding the prohibition of incest. However, the father transmits to her a promise that allows her to wait and receive it from another man when she grows up. The promise is also a symbolic gift offered by the father to his daughter. As we can see, a dialectic of exchange takes place between the father and the daughter, exchange that contains a promise with respect to the possibility of a man other than the father. The phallus is not only the promise of another man but also the key to the identifications with the moral and social ideals represented by the father, ideals from which ensues the formation of the ego ideal. This process is different in the boy, who already possesses the penis but not the phallus. The resolution of the Oedipus complex in the boy is conditioned by his renunciation of the phallus with which he seduces and satisfies his mother on an imaginary level. So, neither the boy nor the girl is the possessor of the phallus to the degree that what counts is not its real but its symbolical value. From puberty on, the boy will face the following challenge: Can he authorize himself to possess the phallus in the sense of its symbolic assumption? To be able to possess it means that he has received it as a gift from the father. The amorous gaze of the father who recognizes his son's masculinity is a gift. While the girl traverses the Oedipus complex, it is important that her wish for a child exists in the form of an unconscious fantasy; however, in the young homosexual the wish for a child had been concretized through the existence of a small boy she had met at a summer resort. This boy, as the object of her attention and care, had provided *real* satisfaction for her. This situation anticipated the violent disturbances that would take place in her when the mother gave birth to a boy.

At this point, we can question why Freud and Lacan conceive the young homosexual's desire to have a child only with the father. With the overdetermination of psychic processes, can we not think that the fantasy to have a child could also be related to the mother? This burning need could also have the significance of having a child with her, but beyond that, to be *her* child. The traumatic experience was provoked when the real child was offered by the father to the mother and this event led to the destruction of the imaginary references that had narcissistically sustained her. By imaginary references, Lacan (1956–1957) emphasizes the illusion that she had of possessing the phallus=child coming from the father. She tried to surmount this frustration by identifying with him from a masculine position. From then on she chose a female object, the lady, who became the object of her passion. Thus, she wanted to give the following message to him: 'You see, I love a woman who does not possess the phallus. I love her not because she has the phallus, but, on the contrary, for what she does not have'. The lady did not possess the phallus and her debasement constituted a lack. So, she loved the lady with 'nothing' in return and the beloved never returned her love. Lacan sees in it the most sublimated and developed form of love to the extent that the young girl offered it without anything in return, as was the case of *courtly love* (*amour courtois*) in the Middle Ages. Lacan, like Freud, considered that this form of love reflected a masculine position. Would this mean that such a developed form of love necessitates a person with high moral values and in that case it could only be a man? We are not far from Freud's conception that women lack a strong and consistent super-ego. 'The super-ego is never so inexorable, so impersonal, so independent of its emotional origins as we require it to be in men' (1925j, p. 257).

The 'fall'

Lacan identifies as the precipitating force of the attempt at suicide the father's rejection of the daughter at the moment he sees her in the company of the lady. Hence, it is the rupture of the narcissistic references that would push her to suicide. It is quite surprising that the threat of the loss of the love–object so poignant in this case does not have a place in Lacan's theory. Lacan's emphasis on the young homosexual's identification with the father's phallus can only be understood if we take into consideration the psychical absence of a loving mother. Six years after his seminar *La relation d'objet*, Lacan re-examines the case of the young homosexual in his seminar *L'angoisse* (1962–1963), which indicates a shift in his approach to the experience of loss. The latter is more connected to a narcissistic injury and less related to the phallus. Lacan focuses here on the father's rejection that had provoked the young girl's 'fall' in narcissistic terms and refers to the signifier *niederkommen* that Freud explains in a footnote. In German, the word means 'to fall'. Lacan emphasizes the violent enactment that characterizes the attempt at suicide of the subject in melancholia, when throwing himself/herself out of the window. But he does not define the young homosexual's enactment as pertaining to melancholia. He considers her hysterical to the extent that she is homosexual, thus establishing a relation between hysteria and homosexuality.

He attributes the young girl's suicide attempt to a 'fall' with respect to object a, the object of desire. What the young girl had perceived in her father's furious glance was that she had been removed from the place she had occupied in his desire. Hence, the anguish caused by it had precipitated her attempt at suicide. Lacan discusses the young girl's 'fall' into a debased position by referring to Freud's use of *niederkommen*. Here, what seems fundamental to us is not the hysterical, that is the sexual sense of the 'fall', but its melancholic sense referring to the loss of the object.

In his seminar *L'angoisse*, Lacan (1962–1963) defines the attempt at suicide of the young homosexual as a *passage à l'acte*, differentiating it from *acting out*. In psychiatric experience the first corresponds to violent enactments such as crime, suicide or sexual aggression, whereas the second is a manifestation of transference. The provocative way in which the young girl exhibited her relation with the lady aimed at hurting her father and corresponded to the transferential aspect of the mechanism of *acting out*. In this sense, transference is not restricted to analysis and can also happen outside. However, in the analytic process the patient's *acting out* requires the analyst's interpretation. Therefore, an *acting out* is subject to interpretation, namely to symbolization, whereas a *passage à l'acte* is the point of rupture of language. In the case of a crime, which is the most extreme situation of the rupture of the symbolic order, the prohibition to kill has to be restored by means of law, that is according to the symbolic order (Legendre, 1989). Lacan defines as a *passage à l'acte* the violent enactment of the melancholic subject, who throws himself/herself out of the window into the void. At this point, he brightly contributes to the discussion. The window constitutes a frontier between the world and the psychic scene, the latter referring to a subject that has a history. Thus, the impulse of the melancholic subject to throw himself/herself out of the window corresponds to the wish to be freed from the weight and burden of the historic scene. In his seminar *L'angoisse*, Lacan argues that by means of enactment, 'the subject returns again to a fundamental exclusion that he/she has experienced in general' (Lacan, 1962–1963, p. 130, my own translation). Let us recall that Freud, in a footnote that he adds to the case of Dora, defines her reluctance to forgive her father as being melancholic. But he remarks that, during analysis, melancholia is treated as hysteria. Freud's discrete remark seems to us important in a discussion on female sexuality because it draws a bridge over the relation between hysteria and melancholia, showing that they share a common aspect pertaining to the feminine.

Time 3: Sidonie Csillag's biography

Freud was not informed about the other two attempts at suicide by the young girl. This situation made it all the more strange, as Freud in general was interested in knowing about the progress or difficulties of his patients after the termination of their analysis. His disinterest with regard to the young girl could only be understood in the light of his resistance related to her homosexuality. Two years after Freud's publication of the case, the young homosexual made a second attempt at suicide. Sidonie, a pseudonym that the authors give to the young homosexual, had begun to feel very unhappy in her relation with Leonie, the real name of the lady. Leonie had left Vienna to meet her lover in Berlin. The despair and sadness that Sidonie felt at that moment were not only due to Leonie's absence, but were also caused by her insensitivity and non-recognition of her feelings. Meanwhile a transformation had occurred in Sidonie, who was no longer disposed towards loving Leonie unconditionally. She needed her love to be reciprocated by the beloved's. In this sense, she was closer to the feminine position when she wished to be loved by Leonie. In that night of 1922, she stole from her friend's handbag a phial that contained poison and ingested it. Sidonie knew that her friend carried it in her bag to use in case the communists came to power. This detail seems ironical to us. It is strange that the high bourgeoisie of Vienna dreaded the communists, when they had no apprehension with respect to Nazism, whose black clouds would cover all of Europe. After having ingested the poison, Sidonie felt very bad, vomiting several times, and thought that she had failed to kill herself like the first time. Contrary to the first attempt at suicide, which was a *passage à l'acte* that had suddenly and violently irrupted into the scene where the father and the lady were present, the other two were premeditated. So, the last two attempts, as an *acting out*, were carriers of a message directed at the beloved. She wanted to show Leonie that her own life was meaningless and worthless without her love and attention. On the other hand, the second and third attempts shared in common the fact that they took place outside her house. She had planned them in such a way that her father would not have to face them and suffer as a result. We can see here how much the young girl was attached to him and cared for him.

After the second attempt, a major event occurred in Sidonie's life that led to a change in her feelings with respect to Leonie. The latter was accused and imprisoned for charges of poisoning and intending to kill her husband. Sidonie, who till then had idealized Leonie, realized how morally degenerate she was. At first, she put all her strength and intelligence into saving her from prison and developed, together with the attorney, a defence strategy that would liberate her. During this process she was interrogated by the police because of her love affair with Leonie and her relationship was made public by the newspapers. After having succeeded in liberating Leonie from prison, she no longer wished to continue her relationship with her and decided to end it. In other words, she was finally able to 'kill' her. We would like to recall Freud's important idea when he claimed that nobody could find the strength to kill themselves unless that person was killing an internal object, a parent that was the object of hate. At this point, Sidonie succeeded in freeing herself from Leonie by 'killing' her and thus did not direct her hate against herself. Did this signify that she was at last able to free herself from the maternal imago? The brutality of the third attempt at suicide shows that the fierce maternal imago continued to represent a powerful force in her psychic reality. The second and third attempts reflected her despair and profound pain. But it was pain without suffering, which, on the contrary, corresponds to an awareness and elaboration of psychic pain, where the condition of such an elaboration is a reflexive position in which the subject can introject it in a masochistic way. In the latter, the pain is not denied but integrated into psychic reality through *erotogenic masochism* (Freud, 1924c), which would assure the binding of pain and unpleasure through the libido. No human being could survive the adversities of life if it were not for the erotogenic masochism, which protects not only against one's own destructivity but also against the aggressions inflicted by the others as a consequence of living in society. Erotogenic masochism has to be differentiated from moral masochism to the degree that the second consists in 'a sense of guilt which is mostly unconscious' (Freud, 1924c, p. 161) and in a loose connection with sexuality. Erotogenic masochism, and feminine masochism deriving from the first, are forms of pain that 'emanate from the loved person', whereas in moral masochism it is the pain itself that matters and is characterized by the destructivity 'raging against the self'.

In order to restore her reputation that had been damaged after her relation with Leonie had been made public, Sidonie decided to enter a circle of young men among whom she met Fritz. The latter produced an intense excitement in her. However, she did not know how to relate to him from a feminine position that was unknown and enigmatic to her. She used to observe with perplexity her mother's seductive behaviour with regard to her husband. Dora (1905e) had sought through Mrs K the answer to the question 'How does one become a woman?'. Sidonie, on the contrary, felt completely lost because she was deprived of a female object of identification. Leonie, with her bad reputation, could not be a model for her. The young girl perceived her mother's femininity as something unfathomable and inaccessible. The girl's femininity can only be built on the basis of a reliable tie to the mother, who is satisfied by having given birth to a girl and can identify her as *her* daughter. For Sidonie, there had been a void at this level as her mother preferred her sons. On the other hand, she was not allowed to share significant moments with her father due to the interference of her mother, who could not tolerate being excluded from her husband's attention. It was impossible to compete with a mother who was so fierce and aggressive. In spite of all her awkwardness, Sidonie nevertheless felt very happy in Fritz's company. But he seemed reluctant to engage himself intimately with her. His distant attitude provoked disappointment in her, in a moment in which she was still in great pain from having lost Leonie. She felt that the object of her desire was again insensitive to her needs.

Another young man named Klaus was very attracted to Sidonie although he knew that she had an inclination for women. When one day Klaus kissed her, she found it very repugnant. By this time she was twenty-five years old and had not yet experienced any sexual relation with men or with women. While Fritz's remoteness saddened her, Klaus's interest awakened her fears with regard to sexuality. When Klaus proposed marriage to her, she accepted it thinking that she could easily impose her wishes on him and have the possibility of meeting a woman under the cover of marriage. Here, it is noteworthy to emphasize the complexity of her psychic reality. At a moment when she was saddened and disappointed by Fritz's remoteness, she was already envisaging the possibility of a marriage that could allow her to meet a woman more freely. Freud had observed this duality or splitting in her when he noted the contradiction between her desire for a man's love as expressed in her dreams, and her plans to get married to a man in order to conceal her homosexual intentions. Freud could not tolerate this manipulative aspect in her and had rejected her by ending her analysis. In fact, this case astounds us by its complexity and uncanny aspects, as her biography indicates. What was revealed to be of great complexity was not only Sidonie's bisexuality, but also this perverse aspect in her psychic functioning. However, as time passed she began to despair about the idea of getting married to a man that she did not love. She thought that her parents would experience great shame if she desisted from her decision of marriage. In a visit to her friends' house she met Fritz and talked to him about their relationship, expressing that she would always love him. When she retired to her bedroom, she took a revolver out of her bag and placed it into her mouth pulling the trigger. But she did not succeed in killing herself as she did not know how to use a revolver. She was immediately hospitalized. After having recovered, she dissolved her engagement with Klaus. She had expected Fritz to visit her in the hospital and was disappointed by his absence. In this sense, the third attempt, like the second one, was an *acting out* that corresponded to a message to the beloved to demonstrate her love. Two years later, Fritz died of medical negligence in a hospital where he had been admitted for the treatment of syphilis. Sidonie was immersed in deep pain and grieved his loss and would frequently visit his tomb. Her parents were astonished at their daughter's affliction. While the anterior tentative of suicide could not be elaborated by her, the loss of Fritz had been capable of provoking a process of mourning. Sidonie had seemed to oscillate, with great dissatisfaction, between female and male love objects till she met Fritz. However, in the case of reciprocated love on Fritz's part, would she be capable of really loving him? By longing for an object that did not manifest his desire for her, was she trying to recreate the disappointment of not having been loved by the maternal object? Was her mode hysterical, as Lacan thought it was? Her relation to the mother was a continuous source of painful dissatisfaction, as the object was distant, cold and oblivious of her needs. The three attempts pointed to the impossibility of being loved and cherished by the object and came to repeat the disappointment with respect to the maternal object. In this sense, it is the mother's love for the daughter that imprints the latter's erotic life, providing her the narcissistic foundation from which she can move to the father (or his substitute) and love him.

References

Cournut, M. (2015). The same and the other: Homosexuality in adolescence. In: E. Abrevaya & F. Thomson-Salo (Eds.), *Homosexualities*. London: Karnac.

Freud, S. (1905d). *Three essays on the theory of sexuality. SE: 7,* 125–245.

Freud, S. (1905e). Fragment of an analysis of a case of hysteria. *SE: 7,* 3–122.

Freud, S. (1910h). A special type of choice of object made by men. *SE: 11,* 165–175.

Freud, S. (1914c). On narcissism: an introduction. *SE: 14,* 73–102.

Freud, S. (1917e). Mourning and melancholia. *SE: 14,* 237–258.

Freud, S. (1919e). A child is being beaten: A contribution to the study of the origin of sexual perversions. *SE: 17,* 179–204.

Freud, S. (1920a). The psychogenesis of a case of homosexuality in a woman. *SE: 18,* 145–172.

Freud, S. (1924c). The economic problem of masochism. *SE: 19,* 159–170.

Freud, S. (1925j). Some psychical consequences of the anatomical distinction between the sexes. *SE: 19,* 248–258.

Freud, S. (1926d). *Inhibitions, symptoms and anxiety. SE: 20,* 77–175.

Freud, S. (1931b). Female sexuality. *SE: 21,* 223–246.

Freud, S. (1933a). Femininity. *New introductory lectures on psycho-analysis. SE: 22:* 112–135.

Horney, K. (1967). *Feminine psychology.* New York: W.W. Norton.

Lacan, J. (1953). Fonction et champ de la parole et du langage en psychanalyse. In: *Ecrits.* Paris: Seuil, 1966.

Lacan, J. (1956–1957). *Le séminaire. Livre IV. La relation d'objet.* Paris: Seuil, 1994.

Lacan, J. (1962–1963). *Le Séminaire. Livre X. L'angoisse.* Paris: Seuil, 2004.

Lacan, J. *Ecrits* (1977). *A selection.* London: W.W. Norton.

Laplanche, J. (2006). *L'après-coup.* Paris: PUF.

Legendre, P. (1989). *Le crime du caporal Lortie. Traité sur le père.* Paris: Fayard.

Masson, J.M. (Ed.) (1985). *The complete letters of Sigmund Freud, to Wilhelm Fliess. 1887–1904.* London: Harvard University Press.

Rieder, I. & Voigt, D. (2004). *Sidonie Csillag. La joven homosexual de Freud.* Buenos Aires: El Cuenco de Plata.

Rosenberg, B. (1991). *Masochisme mortifère et masochisme gardien de la vie.* Paris: PUF.

Young-Bruehl, E. (1991). *Anna Freud.* Paris: Payot.

3 Women analysing women

Focusing on female sexuality from the perspective of the girl's early attachment to the mother confronts the woman analyst with counter-transferential difficulties, which awaken intense affects pertaining to this period. The analytic work requires the capacity to receive and contain them, but also identify and define these affects to the extent that a powerful repression has struck the early phases and created the feeling that they have never existed. In 'Female sexuality', Freud ascertained that the identification of this period presented great difficulties because of a veil that covered it.

> Everything in the sphere of this first attachment to the mother seemed to me so difficult to grasp in analysis – so grey with age and shadowy and almost impossible to revivify – that it was as if it had succumbed to an especially inexorable repression.
>
> (1931b, p. 226)

Another aspect that characterizes analytic work with women, as we observe in supervisions, are the depressive effects induced by the 'sameness' of the members of the analytic couple. The 'sameness' captures the analyst in terms of identification and the work comprises the risk of getting stuck in the narcissistic register, that of separation and loss of the object. The woman analyst's identification with her woman patient's conflicts in the narcissistic sphere tends to provoke a kind of entanglement as well as a blindness with respect to the erotic aspects in the transference. Or, the woman patient's homosexual transference tends to lead to resistances in the woman analyst.

Freud draws our attention to the conflicts provoked by the girl's fixation on the mother. 'Indeed, we have to reckon with the possibility that a number of women remain arrested in their original attachment to their mother and never achieve a true change-over towards men' (1931b, p. 226). Julia Kristeva (2005) underlines the existence of a double love object that confers an interminable, thus, a tortuous oscillation between the maternal object and the paternal object. The girl would oscillate between *Oedipus*

DOI: 10.4324/9781003232261-3

prime, her passion for the mother and *Oedipus again*, the love that has been transferred to the father. Or, the strong attachment to the maternal object provokes endless returns from the father to the mother and makes its elaboration necessary. Kristeva's point of view with respect to the oscillation between the double love object finds an echo in Juliett Michell's conception of femininity. The girl's sexual development creates a complexity as she moves from the mother to the father and this displacement 'makes heterosexuality always a precarious substitute' (Mitchell, 2008, p. xvi).

Helene Deutsch: The *terra incognita*

Freud observed that his women patients clung to their attachment to the father as a refuge in order to avoid the zone of conflicts pertaining to their early attachment. Hence, the paternal transference with its erotic components predominated the analytic scene. At this point we can question to what degree Freud was in a disposition to receive the maternal transference and allow its display on the analytic scene. Female libido was specially unappreciated by Freud and he affirmed in *Three essays* (1905d) that the libido was masculine. He refused to play the role of the mother in the transference and receive the woman patient's affects with respect to the maternal object, work that would have required the contact with his unconscious infantile sexuality. He had precisely failed with Dora when her analysis concerned the transference to Mrs K and also with the young homosexual because he could not manage her passionate love for a woman who was a mother-substitute. However in 'Female sexuality', Freud acknowledged the success of women analysts, such as Lampl-de Groot and Helene Deutsch. Both of them had been able to identify aspects of the early attachment of their women patients, thanks to 'the transference to a suitable mother-substitute' (Freud, 1931b, p. 227).

Or, Helene Deutsch's contribution to female psychology has to be underlined. She had been in analysis with Freud during a year and her husband had been Freud's physician. She was one of the leading training analysts of the Vienna Psychoanalytic Institute and was the first woman analyst to write, in 1925, a book on female psychology, *Psychoanalysis of the sexual functions of women* (1991). Despite the fact that Freud seldom referred to his female disciples' writings, he cited Deutsch's book in 'Some psychical consequences of the anatomical distinction between the sexes' (1925j) as well as in 'Female sexuality' (1931b). It is plausible to think that Freud was influenced and inspired by Deutsch's book, in a moment when he was developing his theory of female sexuality. In the last chapter of her book, Deutsch discusses the question of menopause. It was courageous for a woman psychoanalyst at that time to include it in a book on female sexuality, when we know that a century later women psychoanalysts still tend to ignore it, as it is experienced as a narcissistic injury. However, in spite of her courage to write on menopause, she defined it as the most traumatic experience ever faced by women. The loss of the reproductive capacity as well as the reactivation of the castration complex would provoke catastrophic effects in narcissistic terms. The loss of the genital function is radical and Deutsch uses the term of *dismantlement* to refer to this loss, which leads to a libidinal regression to the phallic phase. The clitoris becomes again, as in childhood, the dominant erotogenic zone leading to the woman's 'masculinity'. In fact, the weakest part of her theory on female sexuality corresponds to her having initiated the feminine drives, like Freud, at the onset of puberty. The sense of deprivation of one own's femininity during menopause creates the feeling that what has come 'too late' has gone 'too early'. Thus, a gap is created between the girl's infantile sexuality and the sexuality experienced from puberty on. However, we know that the girl who has had the assurance of having been loved by both parents but particularly by her father, can, with more ease, overcome the traumatic effects of menopause. Marie-Christine Laznick (2003) notes that women who had a special loving relation with their father during childhood had a better chance of overcoming the effects of menopause.

In a letter to her husband, Helene Deutsch expresses that her book explores the early phases, a *terra incognita*: 'It brings something new to this *terra incognita* in analysis – I believe, the first ray of light on the unappreciated female libido'. Paul Roazen cites these lines in his biography of Helene Deutsch (Roazen, 1985, p. 231). Despite shedding light on female sexuality, an unknown continues to exist in Deutsch's theory to the extent that the little girl's feminine drives with respect to the father as well as her conflicts with regard to the mother are left in the dark. It is Melanie Klein who will establish the map of the young child's unconscious fantasies with respect to both the maternal and paternal objects. The notion of *terra incognita* connects us to a contemporary text of Gerhard Schneider, who uses this metaphor to define the traces of early experiences that constitute a sense of identity but are not apparently identifiable. 'In other words, we are confronted with a part of the psyche that is conspicuous by its absence' (Schneider, 2014, p. 31). The part of the psyche that concerns the girl's early identification with the mother is fundamental in the constitution of female subjectivity and acquires a special value in the analysis of women. It is necessary that the sphere of the girl's early attachment be 'mapped out', giving us the key to the passionate love for the mother but also to her feminine drives with respect to the father. The inaccessibility of the early phases is not only due to the inexorable character of repression but is equally related to the woman analyst's resistances. Helene Deutsch ascertained that resistances arose from women analysts, who surprisingly could not appreciate 'the female libido'. She dared to speak of 'female libido' in spite of her loyalty to Freud, who defended the opposite. Her findings were followed by those of Karen Horney (1926), Ernest Jones (1927, 1933, 1935), Melanie Klein (1928, 1932) and Freud (1931b, 1933a). In a time when Freud's conception of female sexuality centred on the phallus, analysts like Otto Rank, Georg Groddeck and Sandor Ferenczi attached importance to the analyst who played the mother's role in the transference. 'Helene was the one analyst, however, to look at motherhood primarily from the perspective of its significance for female psychology' (Roazen, 1985, p. 235).

The father as the object of the girl's feminine drives

The mother, who takes care and satisfies the child's necessities, has a primordial role in her psychic development. However, motherhood is not exempt from eroticism. She has a sexual life with the father (or the lover). The little girl identifies with the femininity of her mother, whose object of desire is the father (or the lover) and perceives from very early on that there is an object other than her for the mother. The latter necessarily communicates to her child her unconscious sexual fantasies, which become the source of sexual excitation. Hence, she becomes the first seducer of the child. Freud remarks:

> A child's intercourse with anyone responsible for his care affords him an unending source of sexual excitation and satisfaction from his erotogenic zones. This is especially so since the person in charge of him, who, after all, is as rule his mother, herself regards him with feelings that are derived from her own sexual life: she strokes him, kisses him, rocks him and quite clearly treats him as a substitute for a complete sexual object.
>
> (1905d, p. 223)

In *New foundations for psychoanalysis* (1991), Jean Laplanche speaks of an original passivity due to the helplessness of the newborn, whose necessities require the indispensable presence of an adult who can bring comfort and satisfy the needs. However, the bodily care given by the mother is never transparent and is always a vehicle for enigmatic messages that refer to her unconscious sexual fantasies. The mother is not aware that her affection and care arouse sexual excitement and she 'innocently' seduces her child. Jean Laplanche's theory of general seduction is precisely founded on the libidinal relation that the mother establishes with her child. The mother's unconscious fantasies focus on the erotogenic zones of her child, provoking sexual excitation in the form of a *foreign internal body* (Breuer & Freud, 1895d; Laplanche, 1985). The excitation is introduced through the orifices, such as the mouth, the anus, and the vagina in the case of the girl. The child faces the necessity of treating the excitation to which he/she has been subjected in a passive position. However, what is decisive in the constitution of the girl's femininity is the mother's desire for the paternal object. In his seminar *Les formations de l'inconscient* (1957–1958), Jacques Lacan introduces the mother's desire for the phallus at the foundation of the Oedipus complex. The mother's body is not only excited by her child, but also by her erotic fantasies with respect to the lover. In order to experience a sexual union with the lover and become again a woman with him, she temporarily retires her investment and exercises a 'censorship' by putting her child to sleep. Denise Braunschweig and Michel Fain (1975) define the 'censorship of the lover', whose aim is to protect the child from the mother's sexual excitement aroused by the father (or the lover). The temporary absence of the mother creates the possibility of a hysteric identification with her and the perception that her desire as a woman points to an object other than himself/herself. Thus, a representation with regard to the third can be configured and curiosity with respect to 'the other of the object' (Green, 2004) can be established. By putting her child to sleep, the mother allows the constitution of a division in the child's psyche between night and day and between the unconscious and the conscious, division in which Braunschweig and Fain situate the origin of psychic life. The young child's identification with the mother who desires the father (or the lover), introduces from the very beginning the place of the father as the third, rendering viable the constitution of the Oedipus complex as a ternary, that is a symbolic structure.

Lacan and the Oedipus complex

Lacan conceives the Oedipus complex in three phases, as he parts from a triangle formed by the child, the mother and the father. In his theory there is no such thing as 'the pre-oedipal' to the extent that the child is born into an oedipal structure. The access to the oedipal structure is conditioned by the place that the child occupies in the parent's unconscious fantasy. The child can, for example, occupy the place of a dead brother or sister, or can be identified with the madness or the incapacitating condition of a close relative of the mother. However, it would be too simple to imagine that the child becomes what the parent unconsciously wants of him or of her. As the analytical experience shows, the child's position with respect to the preconscious/unconscious messages coming from the parent is equally essential. Does the child identify with what he/she perceives as being the mother's desire? Is it too threatening for a boy to reclaim his masculinity when the mother assigns him the place of a girl? Can the girl allow herself to be feminine when the preconscious messages coming from the mother prohibit it? This was the case of the young homosexual, as the mother saw in her daughter a rival that had to be fought against.

Lacan names the first phase in which the child identifies with the object of the mother's desire as the 'primitive phallic phase'. Even if the father cannot yet be differentiated from the mother, he is effective because he represents the symbolic order. The child perceives the lack of the phallus in the mother and wishes to complement her. Lacan distinguishes between the penis as an organ and the phallus consisting in a psychic representation based on the erect penis. But penis-envy does not refer to the penis as the organ but to its psychic representation in the woman's unconscious fantasy. However, the phallus in Lacan's theory is more than a representation. It is a signifier that plays a pivotal role permitting the relations between the child, the mother and the father in each stage of the Oedipus complex to be examined. In the second phase, the father prevents the mother from integrating her product, that is from returning the child to her womb, and gives at the same time the message to the child that he/she cannot possess the mother. Lacan is interested in the symbolic effect of privation on the child. The father's prohibition with respect to the sexual union with the mother gives the child the possibility of liberating himself or herself from the illusion of satisfying the mother. Lacan names this phase 'central and negative' to the extent that the father, by his prohibition, represents a negative function. Submitting to the mother's caprices and desires impedes the child from becoming a subject. Even if the child wishes to satisfy the mother with regard to her lack of phallus, there is, however, a lack that the child can never fill and that corresponds to the object of her desire. In the third phase, the father's intervention as the possessor of the phallus leads to the child's identification with him and the possibility of perceiving that he is the only one who can offer her the satisfaction of her desire. At this point, the identification with the father assures the resolution of the incestual tendencies and leads to the formation of the ego ideal. Thus, the archaic paternal function that can operate thanks to the mother's desire for the father (Kristeva, 2003) at the beginning of the child's life constitutes the foundation of the ego ideal, which can only be effective in the third phase.

We have seen that it is the mother's desire for the father that allows the paternal function to operate and points to an object beyond the child that precisely causes her desire. The burning desire for the object is relative not only to the penis but also to the love for the man who possesses the penis. Hence, we accord to the mother a pivotal role in terms of the effectiveness of the paternal function, an aspect that permits us to question the Lacanian concept of the 'symbolic father' as an absolute and unchangeable structure. In 'Thirdness and psychoanalytic concepts', André Green draws our attention to the way the father is experienced in the mother's psychic reality:

> But a true psychoanalytic investigation – not an ethological one – should consider *where and how* the father is experienced in the mother's mind at this stage of intimacy between mother and child. One might even pose the query, 'Who is the true father for the mother? Is it her own father, her mother, a brother, an earlier lover?'.
>
> (2004, p. 104)

The mother's face and body reflect her desire for the object. Or, we know that for Winnicott (1971) the mother's face reflects her affects with respect to the child but nothing about her womanly desire for the father (or the lover). André Green (2004) refers to the father (or the lover) as 'the mother's other' but the other also corresponds to the symbolic and cultural order. The mother is not an isolated being; on the contrary, she is inserted in the cultural world. She can raise her child without the presence of the real father, thanks to the existence of a symbolic and cultural order, as well as to her relation with her father (or the father-substitutes). On the other hand, the third can also be represented by a lover having the same sex with her, as long as each partner of the couple is psychically differentiated from the other. In this case, it is the psychic *difference* between the partners that is the symbolic operator (André, 2015).

The beating-fantasy

'A child is being beaten' (1919e) is a text that illustrates the femininity of the little girl with respect to the father. Both Dora's case and this text constitute a treasure for the understanding of the little girl's incestual fantasies. In the centre of this text lies a genital fantasy that has been repressed and can only be revealed by analysis. In this sense, the beating-fantasy would be 'precipitates of the Oedipus complex, scars, so to say, left behind after the process has ended' (Freud, 1919e, p. 193). It corresponds to a typical feminine fantasy in which the father is the erotic object. In 1915 Freud adds a footnote to *Three essays on the theory of sexuality* (1905d) in which he discusses the transformations of puberty, which leads to a 'sharp' distinction between the masculine and the feminine. However, there is no such thing as pure masculinity or pure femininity in men and women respectively. On the contrary, as part of their psychic bisexuality, they display a mixture of masculine and feminine attitudes.

> Every individual on the contrary displays a mixture of the character-traits belonging to his own and to the opposite sex; and he shows a combination of activity and passivity whether or not these last character-traits tally with his biological ones.
>
> (1905d, pp. 219–220)

In the beating-fantasy, both the girl and the boy are placed in a passive position with respect to the seduction of the erotic object, the father. The beating-fantasy that had appeared in the material of Freud's analysands did not mean that they had really been beaten in their childhood. They had probably observed a child being beaten by a teacher in school. In this sense, the presence of a strong parental character comes to emphasize the child's passivity in the fantasy. Who is the author of the fantasy, the one who builds the fantasy or is it another child? Who is the adult that is beating? Freud examines the fantasy in three phases. The first phase refers to scenes where the girl has seen another child being beaten and is expressed with this phrase: '*My father is beating the child*'. The author of the fantasy participates in the scene by observing it. This representation is not a fantasy yet, but is its precursor. This phrase in the course of analysis is transformed into: 'My father is beating the child *whom I hate*'. The fantasy is of sadistic nature and the child who is being beaten is the younger brother or sister with whom the girl competes for the father's love. The fantasy comprises three actors: the father who beats, hence punishes, the young brother or sister subject to his punishment and the girl who participates by watching it. The beating of the younger brother or sister is an indicator that the girl is the preferred one and the scene provokes guilt. In this sense, the father seems to show his preference and love for his daughter, hence becoming seductive with her.

In the second phase, only two actors figure, the father and the girl. Thanks to the transformation between the first and the second phases, the child being beaten becomes now the author of the fantasy. '*I am being beaten by my father*' is of a masochistic nature and is repressed because it is tinted with a high degree of pleasure. At this point, it becomes possible to conceive a fantasy because the sexual drive has been repressed and has returned to the ego in the form of a fantasy. In *Essays on otherness* (Laplanche & Fletcher, 1998), Laplanche remarks that the sexual is not the drive itself but the *unconscious fantasy* whose presence means that repression has operated. Hence, repression of the sexual drive allows the differentiation of the psychic apparatus into the unconscious and the preconscious/conscious. The second phase is the most important of the three phases. The father's beating now acquires the signification of loving the daughter. 'My father does not love this other child, *he loves only me*'. The girl's feeling is that his father loves her by beating her and he beats her because he loves her. Being beaten by the father acquires the signification of being penetrated by him and having coitus, which provoke guilt. 'This beating is now a convergence of the sense of guilt and sexual love. *It is not only the punishment for the forbidden genital relation, but also the regressive substitute for that relation*' (1919e, p. 189, original emphasis). As the desire to be penetrated is highly erotic, it succumbs not only to repression but also undergoes a regression from the genital phase to the sadistic–anal phase. The beating-fantasy in its masochistic form is the regressive expression of being genitally loved by the father and can only be revealed thanks to analysis. The desire to be beaten, that is to be penetrated by the father, will equally be valid for the boy. Each time it concerns a feminine position. The third phase presents a similitude with the first phase. As a result of repression, the adult who is beating becomes a substitute for the father and the author of the fantasy does not figure in the scene. As the scene is related to the second phase, it is clearly sexual and a vehicle for intense sexual excitement in the girl, provoking the need for masturbation. The beating-fantasy indicates to what degree the girl's femininity is related to the desire for the father. In this sense, it is not conceivable to consider her femininity as being 'natural', as Melanie Klein and Ernest Jones defend it.

The girl's 'natural' femininity

Contrary to the approach that accords a key function to the father both as a libidinal object and a symbolic object, Melanie Klein's and Ernest Jones' conception of femininity is based on the girl's instinctual make-up. Despite Ernest Jones defining in 'Early female sexuality' (1935) the little girl's desire to incorporate the paternal penis as an expression of an authentic feminine love, her orientation towards the father would still be part of her instinctual make-up. The little girl's femininity is manifested by her desire to incorporate the paternal penis, first orally and later through her vagina. Both Melanie Klein and Ernest Jones situate the girl's primitive feminine drives in the oral phase. In 'The early development of female sexuality' (1927), Ernest Jones remarks that his analysis of adult patients as well as Melanie Klein's analysis of children, along with Freud's findings on the phallic stage, indicate that 'there are more direct transitions between the oral and the Oedipus stages' (1927, p. 463). The oral frustration with respect to the breast becomes the cause of the displacement from the breast to the paternal penis, which is fantasized as being inside the mother's body. At this stage, the breast and the penis as part objects represent the mother and the father. The girl wishes to suck the paternal penis and keep it inside her, as the genital drives accompanying her oral tendencies have a receptive character. Her erotogenic zones, such as the mouth, the anus and the vagina, are excited by the paternal penis. The girl feels a much stronger need than the boy to incorporate the paternal penis due to its libidinal attraction. The incorporation of the paternal penis is facilitated by the receptive character of her oral, anal and genital drives. The wish to acquire a penis by swallowing it and retain it in the body in order to make a baby, gives way to penis-envy, that is to the girl's early wish to possess a penis.

In 'The flight from womanhood' (1926), Karen Horney defines penis-envy at this stage as being primary. It is based on the discovery of sexual difference and has an auto-erotic function related to urethral erotism and the scoptophilic drive. Ernest Jones, like Karen Horney, considers that primary penis-envy takes place prior to the resolution of the Oedipus complex and should be distinguished from the post-oedipal penis-envy corresponding to the complex of masculinity. The latter consists of one of the three solutions that the girl finds at the moment of the resolution of the Oedipus complex. Freud identifies two other solutions, one is a neurotic compromise between sexual pleasure and its prohibition and the other is the feminine solution consisting in the pleasure of being penetrated by the penis. However, primary penis-envy does not represent a conflict with respect to the girl's feminine drives. On the contrary, it is the force that orients her towards the father and in this sense, is positive. Both Lacan and Karen Horney coincide with respect to the positive role played by penis-envy. However, the little girl's orientation towards the father can take place with the condition that he is the mother's object of desire. Penis-envy can later evolve into 'the wish to share his penis in some coitus-like action by means of the mouth, anus or vagina' (Jones, 1927, p. 464). Jones, who situates the prototype of the girl's femininity in the oral drives, considers that the wish to incorporate a penis in order to make a baby is very close to the adult woman's eroticism. In the following months, the little girl perceives the excitement in the cavity in her genital region and has the fantasy that the cavity can receive the penis. Hence, there is a libidinal displacement from 'the upper to the lower' part of her body, that is from the mouth to the vagina. The strong wish to incorporate the paternal penis, which is the object of admiration for its potency to give babies, renders the little girl more vulnerable than the boy to the super-ego's imperatives in her relation to the mother.

The girl's aggressive fantasy consisting in the dispossession of all the 'good' contents in the maternal body provokes anxiety and guilt, hence the apprehension of the mother's retaliation. The fear of having destroyed the very source of her libidinal satisfaction has a great impact in her psychic life. At this point, we can infer that the little girl has already attained the depressive position. But there is an oscillation between the paranoid–schizoid position and the depressive position. She fears that the 'bad' object's retaliation is directed against the interior of her body, particularly the vagina and the uterus, as organs that symbolize fertility. We can question to what extent the little girl can have a representation about the uterus at this stage of her psychic development. Florence Guignard (1999) brings an answer to it. In the geography of the little girl's unconscious fantasies, the uterus of the mother occupies a special place. She envies not only the richness inside the maternal body but also her mother's capability to make babies. Contrary to the boy who can verify that his penis is intact and therefore have an idea that the inside of his body is not damaged, the girl has no such possibility. The fear of retaliation renders her prone to anxiety and guilt, having consequences on the development of her ego and her relations with the objects. Melanie Klein remarks that her aggressive fantasies and the fear of retaliation create the need for reparation, which leads to a strong attachment to the mother, as well as to sublimations in her relations with the objects.

In *The psycho-analysis of children* (1932), Melanie Klein notes that the little girl's wish to possess the paternal penis has neither to do with the appropriation of the father's virility nor is the consequence of penis-envy, but is the *direct* expression of her feminine drives manifested under the dominance of her instinctual feminine tendencies. Ernest Jones will also speak of a 'natural' femininity in the girl, in identification with the mother. However, we know that nothing in human sexuality is 'natural' or 'instinctual'. In *Life and death in psychoanalysis* (1985), Laplanche defines the sexual drive as a deviation from the instinct. The unconscious fantasies of the parent(s) leave their mark on the child's psyche. The 'fundamental anthropological situation' refers to the encounter between the young child and the adult, who already has a sexual life. The adult's unconscious sexual fantasies convey enigmatic messages that the child has to translate and symbolize by means of the sexual theories. However, Ernest Jones makes a notable theoretical shift by differentiating 'natural' femininity in identification with the mother from 'true feminine love' for the father. In spite of the girl's identification with the mother, it would be impossible to conceive a femininity which does not pass by the libidinal desire for the father. We would add that the father's tenderness and love for his daughter is also essential for her femininity. But the girl's femininity with respect to the father has a price. The mother, her oedipal rival, is also a primordial object that she can never risk losing. Moreover, the mother is fundamental for her identity as a girl and later as a woman. Both Karen Horney and Ernest Jones affirm that the appropriation of the feminine drive requires courage, even audacity when it is so guilt-ridden with respect to the mother.

> Horney has pointed out that for a girl to maintain a feminine position and to accept the absence of a penis in herself often signifies not only daring to have incestuous object-wishes, but also the phantasy that her physical state is the result of a castrating rape once actually performed by the father.
>
> (Jones, 1927, p. 468)

In spite of her deep attachment to the mother, the girl has to have the courage to orientate herself to the father and be able to face conflicts with respect to the maternal object. Or, the girl can undertake such a process with the condition of having established a satisfying and confident relation with the mother. Otherwise, the narcissistic ground from which she has to go to the father is shaky and impedes her from entering into a relation of rivalry with the mother. Ernest Jones, very interestingly, arrives at a point where he comes to question his own idea of a 'natural' femininity: Is one born as a woman or becomes a woman? Twenty years later, in *The second sex* Simone de Beauvoir brings, from a social perspective, an answer to this interrogation. 'One is not born, but rather becomes a woman' (de Beauvoir, 2014).

The phallic phase at the resolution of the oedipal complex

At the peak of her erotic desire for the father, the little girl has to make a choice between her father and her femininity. In order to maintain her feminine drives without having to suffer their total extinction (*aphanisis*), she has to renounce the incestual object, which is the only way in which her feminine drives can develop on an adult level and be transferred to another masculine object. Ernest Jones considers that it is the dread of being deprived of the permanent capacity to experience pleasure that leads to the renunciation of the father as a libidinal object. *Aphanisis* is manifested differently in both sexes. While the boy experiences this dread in the form of castration, the girl apprehends it in the form of loss of the object's love.

> Whereas with the male this is typically conceived of in the active form of castration, with the female the primary fear would appear to be that of separation. This can be imagined as coming about through the rival mother intervening between the girl and the father, or even through her sending the girl away for ever, or else through the father simply withholding the desired gratification.
>
> (Jones, 1927, p. 462)

At the XII International Psychoanalytical Association's Congress in Wiesbaden in 1932, Ernest Jones proposed the term of 'phallic phase' to account for the solution that the child finds to the incestual tendencies. Thanks to the vaginal sensations, the little girl perceives that she has a cavity that can be penetrated, whereas the boy perceives that the mother has an orifice other than the mouth and the anus that can be penetrated. At the point of the highest intensity of his incestual desires, the boy wishes, like the father, to penetrate the mother, but he is confronted with the threat of castration represented by him. In order to protect himself against such a threat, he represses his desire for penetration and regresses to the belief of the universality of the phallus. The phallic phase serves as a defence against the incestual tendencies and involves a temporary regression in the child's sexual development. This regression consists in a neurotic compromise that assures the denial of the vagina in both sexes, that is the denial of sexual difference. On this point, Karen Horney concurs with Ernest Jones and remarks that in the girl the neurotic compromise concerns a regression to the phase of primary penis-envy. However, primary penis-envy had originally orientated the little girl from the mother to the father. In other words, the discovery of the father, both as the possessor of the penis and as the object of the mother's desire, had been the motive of the little girl's orientation to the father. That is why Horney remarks that the phallic identification is a regression to the preliminary stage of the oedipal love for the father. The regression to primary penis-envy becomes necessary as the girl's feminine wishes are strongly under the impact of her guilt feelings and anxiety. It is impossible to grasp the girl's feminine wishes with respect to the father without taking into consideration her guilt and anxiety with respect to the mother. The hostility with regard to the mother that the little girl represses and returns to herself can become the cause of her dependency and impede her detachment from the object. However, the boy has the facility to displace the aggression with respect to the mother onto the father, who is the object of rivalry. Contrary to Freud, who affirms the impossibility of the total resolution of the female Oedipus complex because of the lack of castration anxiety in the girl, Melanie Klein (1928, 1932) and Ernest Jones (1927, 1933, 1935) defend the opposite. The fear of retaliation and the threat of losing the mother's love open the way to the definitive resolution of her incestual tendencies and this is due to the force of the super-ego in her. For Melanie Klein the girl's hostility with respect to the mother is the force that creates the need for reparation as well as for investment of the object.

Karen Horney and Ernest Jones conceive the girl's phallic identification as a temporary phase before the onset of puberty, whereas Freud proposes another approach to it. Her libidinal tie to the father becomes the force that underpins her identification with him at the resolution of the Oedipus complex. As the girl renounces her incestual drives, she identifies with the father. However, she does not become a man like him to the degree that she identifies with the signs represented by him. 'The ego ideal is therefore the heir of the Oedipus complex, and thus it is also the expression of the most powerful impulses and most important libidinal vicissitudes of the id' (Freud, 1923b, p. 36). Here, the ego ideal appears as a synonym of the super-ego. However, Laplanche (1980) considers that the ego ideal should be differentiated from the super-ego to the extent that the first tries to harmonize the libidinal exigencies with the cultural exigencies, aspect that is illustrated by sublimation. The identification with the father contributes to the constitution of the girl's ego ideal, which becomes the key in the development of female sexuality as well as in her participation in the cultural world. Even if Freud posits that the identification with the father is due to the force of the child's masculine tendencies in both sexes and this affirmation is true to a certain extent, the identification with him can only derive its force from the child's love and admiration for him. In the case of the boy, it concerns his homosexual love for him. The boy loves his father but also desires to be loved by him. Hence, the desire to be loved that Freud attributes to the woman's narcissism places both the girl and the boy in a feminine position with respect to the father. What seems central in the girl's identification with the father is that it derives its force from her love for him and is founded on her femininity. In other words, it does not consist in her orientation to the father as the possessor of the penis. On the contrary, her femininity on which this identification is grounded implies that the little girl has already experienced her incestual tendencies with respect to the father and has renounced them. In this sense, the identification with the father appears at the culmination of the Oedipus complex.

References

André, J. (2015). Male homosexuality in analytic treatment. In: E. Abrevaya & F. Thomson-Salo (Eds.), *Homosexualities*. London: Karnac.

Braunschweig, D. & Fain, M. (1975). *La nuit et le jour. Essai psychanalytique sur le fonctionnement mental*. Paris: PUF.

Breuer, J. & Freud, S. (1895d). *Studies on hysteria. SE, 2*: 3–305.

De Beauvoir, S. (2014). *The second sex*. New York: Vintage.

Deutsch, H. (1991). *Psychoanalysis of sexual functions of women*. London: Routledge.

Freud, S. (1905d). *Three essays on the theory of sexuality. SE, 7*: 125–245.

Freud, S. (1919e). A child is being beaten. *SE, 17*: 179–204.

Freud, S. (1923b). *The ego and the id. SE, 19*: 12–59.

Freud, S. (1925j). Some psychical consequences of the anatomical distinction between the sexes. *SE: 19*, 243–258.

Freud, S. (1931b). Female sexuality. *SE, 21*: 225–243.

Freud, S. (1933a). Femininity. In: *New introductory lectures on psychoanalysis. SE, 22*: 112–135.

Green, A. (2004). Thirdness and psychoanalytic concepts. *Psychoanalytic quarterly, 73*, 99–135.

Guignard, F. (1999). Maternel ou féminin? Le 'roc d'origine' comme gardien du tabou de l'inceste avec la mère. In: J. Schaeffer, M. Cournut-Janin, S. Faure-Pragier & F. Guignard (Eds.), *Clés pour le féminin*. Paris: PUF.

Horney, K. (1926). The flight from womanhood: The masculinity-complex in women as viewed by men and women. *International journal of psychoanalysis, 7*, 324–339.

Jones, E. (1927). The early development of female sexuality. *International journal of psychoanalysis, 5*, 50–65.

Jones, E. (1933). The phallic phase. *International journal of psychoanalysis, 14*, 1–33.

Jones, E. (1935). Early female sexuality. *International journal of psychoanalysis, 16*, 263–273.

Klein, M. (1928). Early stages of the Oedipus conflict. *International journal of psychoanalysis, 9*, 169–180.

Klein, M. (1932). The effects of early anxiety-situations on the sexual development of the girl. *The psycho-analysis of children*. London: Hogarth.

Kristeva, J. (2003). Le père imaginaire. In: C. Geissman & D. Houzel (Eds.), *L'enfant, ses parents et le psychanalyste*. Paris: Bayard Compact.

Kristeva, J. (2005). La fatigue au féminin. *La haine et le pardon*. Paris: Fayard.

Lacan, J. (1957–1958). *Le séminaire. Livre V. Les formations de l'inconscient*. Paris: PUF, 1998.

Laplanche, J. (1970). *Vie et mort en psychanalyse*. Paris: Flammarion.

Laplanche, J. (1980). *La sublimation*. Paris: PUF.

Laplanche, J. (1985). *Life and death in psychoanalysis*. Baltimore, MD: The John Hopkins University Press.

Laplanche, J. (1991). *New foundations for psychoanalysis*. Cambridge, MA: Basil Blackwell.

Laplanche, J. & Fletcher, J. (1998). *Essays on otherness*. London: Routledge.

Laznik, M.C. (2003). *L'impensable désir. Féminité et sexualité au prisme de la ménopause*. Paris: Denoël.

Mitchell, J. (2008). Foreword. In: J. Raphael-Leff & R. Jozef Perelberg (Eds.), *Female experience: Four generations of British women psychoanalysts on work with women*. London: Anna Freud Centre.

Roazen, P. (1985). *Helene Deutsch*. New York: New American Library.

Schneider, G. (2014). Incisions, rifts, islands. Towards a psychoanalytic topography of psychic states of remoteness and their (un)reachability. *Psychoanalysis in Europe, 68*, 19–36.

Winnicott, D.W. (1971). Mirror-role of mother and family in child development. In: *Playing and reality*. London: Tavistock Publications.

4 The daughter's crucial challenge

Separation

Primary homosexuality

What is it that characterizes the girl's early attachment to the mother and confers its specificity, differentiating it from that of the boy? Evelyn Kestemberg (1984) proposes the term 'primary homosexuality' to designate the relation of the child of both sexes to the first object of love and identification. But, this mode of relation would in a privileged way apply to the girl, who is sexually built like the mother. Similarity with the mother acquires its true value when she discovers sexual difference and perceives that she possesses the same sex with the mother. Till the discovery of sexual difference, the girl's primary identification with the mother has principally a narcissistic value. However, after the recognition of sexual difference, the mother becomes the object of sexual identification. Kestemberg considers that at the beginning both primary identification and primary homosexuality coincide, with sometimes the feeling of the identical prevailing, sometimes that of the mother's otherness. The feeling of being identical ensues from primary identification, whereas that of otherness is relative to primary homosexuality. All the psychic work elaborated around primary homosexuality consists essentially in organizing the relation to the other, eventually to the similar but never to the identical, work that is realized by means of the corporal exchanges between the mother and the child. In primary identification the narcissistic and auto-erotic aspects prevail over the relation to the object, whereas in primary homosexuality it is the libidinal investment of the object that counts most. Women analysts, such as Monique Cournut-Janin, Jacqueline Godfrind and Sylvie Faure-Pragier discuss the conflicted forms of primary homosexuality, which are manifested in the 'black version of the feminine' (Cournut-Janin, 1998, 1999) or in the 'black pact' (Godfrind 2001, 2018). In fact, the 'black version of the feminine' consists in a disturbance that impedes differentiation from the object and it is in the violence and hatred of the homosexual transference that certain aspects of the girl's early attachment are revealed. This is a problematic that we will examine in this chapter, in articulation with Ms Aisha's clinical case.

DOI: 10.4324/9781003232261-4

Paul Denis (1982, 2005) underlines the genetical aspect and developmental sequence of this process, in which primary homosexuality is situated in a period that goes from primary identification to the recognition of sexual difference. Here, the prefix 'homos' refers to the partner's similarity to the child. The passage from primary identification to primary homosexuality involves the transformation of the feeling of unity with the object into that of otherness, an aspect that Evelyn Kestemberg also emphasizes. In primary identification the object is perceived without 'an affect of difference' (Kestemberg, 1984) and the satisfaction is auto-erotic. In opposition to it, in primary homosexuality the child perceives the difference with the object and invests it libidinally. The recognition of sexual difference ends primary homosexuality bringing along a 'Copernican re-organization' (Denis, 2005) of the child's sexuality and culminates in the development of psychic bisexuality, which according to Freud (1923a) is a consequence of the resolution of the Oedipus complex. Hence, the oedipal resolution leads to a double identification, masculine and feminine. In this sense, Denis (2005) establishes an opposition between primary homosexuality concerning undifferentiated sexuality and psychic bisexuality that consists of a double identification with the parents, who are now sexually differentiated. At this point, the fantasy of the primal scene refers to the parental couple composed of the father and the mother, who are sexually differentiated, in opposition to the Kleinian concept of the fantasy of combined parents.

The mother establishes an affective, sensual and sensuous relation with her baby and in this sense primary homosexuality applies to the child of both sexes and consists in the mark of the feminine on the psyche. The boy, like the girl, identifies with the primary object and this is the *reason why the feminine element has at the beginning a dominant influence on him. However,* the feminine element is not limited to the early phase. During the oedipal situation, the feminine position of the boy in regard to the father will also play a key role, along with his desire with respect to the mother. It is evident that even when we speak of primary homosexuality, it includes from the very beginning the object of the mother's desire, the father or the lover. Having the same body and genitals with the mother has the effect of a psychic impregnation on the girl's body image. A young woman patient questioned why her mother had projected her own problematic to her and not to her brother. Her mother, who had undergone several abortions, had projected her conflicts onto her daughter. The latter attributed them to having the same body and sex: 'I imagine it is because I have a vagina'.

The introjection of the object

While Kestemberg and Denis refer to primary identification in order to designate the early forms of objectal love, Kristeva (1987) proposes instead the term 'introjection'. The young child introjects the object in the form of a bodily fusion, in a time that is inaccessible to words and memories. It was Ferenczi (1909) who used the term introjection for the first time in 1909, in his essay 'Introjection and transference' to describe the neurotic's tendency to transfer to the physician the affects that are conflicted, hence avoiding having an insight into their unconscious source. In opposition to the paranoiac who expels the impulses that cause him displeasure, the neurotic *takes into the ego the largest possible part of the outer world, rendering it the object of* unconscious phantasies. Ferenczi sees the paranoiac's tendency to project the impulses that cause displeasure and the neurotic's inclination to introject as extreme cases of psychic processes, whose primary forms can be observed in every human being. Hence, 'the first loving and hating' is a transference of pleasant and unpleasant feelings onto the objects that awaken these feelings. This idea anticipates Freud's point of view with respect to the opposition between the subject (ego) and the object (external world) on one hand and between pleasure and unpleasure on the other hand, aspects that he will examine in 'Instincts and their vicissitudes' (1915c). At the beginning of psychic life, the external world cannot be invested and this is due to the investment of the ego with drives that satisfy themselves auto-erotically. 'During this period, therefore, the ego-subject coincides with what is pleasurable and the external world with what is indifferent (or possibly unpleasurable, as being a source of stimulation)' (1915c, p. 135). Later, under the dominance of the pleasure principle, the ego undergoes a new development.

> In so far as the objects which are presented to it are sources of pleasure, it takes them into itself, 'introjects' them (to use Ferenczi's [1909] term); and on the other hand, it expels whatever within itself becomes a cause of unpleasure.
>
> (1915c, pp. 135–136)

Ferenczi re-examines the notion of introjection in 1912. By means of the introduction of the external objects into the ego, interest is extended to the external world. *Objectal love* (or *transference*) is an extension of the ego.

The term introjection plays an important role equally both in Karl Abraham's (1924) and Melanie Klein's (1932) works. In her effort to understand the child's relation to the maternal body, Melanie Klein resorts to the notions of unconscious fantasy and anxiety. As a result of the aggressive fantasies that the child directs at the mother's body, the object becomes dangerous and capable of reprisals. So, the child is forced to 'transfer' (Ferenczi, 1909) his or her interest to objects less dangerous in the external world. 'Thus through symbolization his interest in his mother's body begins to extend to the whole world around him' (Segal, 1974, p. 5). In other words, by displacing his or her interest to objects that are less dangerous, the child introjects the good object, projects the bad object and then re-introjects them. This process corresponds to symbol-formation.

While a certain amount of anxiety is the force underlying these displacements, its excessive amount detains the symbolization process, as illustrated by the case of Dick, an autistic child suffering from mutism that Melanie Klein treated in 1930. In his seminar *Les écrits techniques de Freud* (1953–1954), Lacan discusses the clinical genius of Melanie Klein, who introduces into Dick's psychic reality the first symbols of the Oedipus complex. Hence, Dick begins to utter the first words and to extend his interest to the objects in his environment, by proceeding from what are internally fantasized as dangerous objects to less dangerous ones outside. Both Ferenczi and Lacan agree that the child's psychic reality is constituted by the introjection of the external objects, in a process that progressively allows the display and use of a greater number of objects.

In *The language of psychoanalysis* (1988), Laplanche and Pontalis defend the necessity to differentiate between the terms introjection and incorporation, a position that is also adopted by Lacan (1964) and Torok (1987). Both Laplanche and Pontalis remark that incorporation refers to a corporal envelope separating the interior from the exterior and at the beginning it is in the oral mode that the object is incorporated or expelled. They identify three main significations of incorporation: 1. To give pleasure to oneself by introducing the object into the body. 2. Destroy the object. 3. Assimilate the qualities of the object by maintaining it inside oneself. This last aspect constitutes the matrix of introjection and identification. The authors make an important distinction when they posit that introjection does not only mark the corporal frontier between the interior and the exterior as in the case of incorporation, but also indicates the interior of the psychic apparatus or the interior of an agency. Hence, the interior of the psychic apparatus can refer to the introjection of the good object *into the ego* and this is Ferenzci's emphasis in 1912. In his seminar *Les quatre concepts fondamentaux de la psychanalyse* (1964), Lacan coincides with Laplanche and Pontalis when he refers to introjection as a symbolic process, in opposition to incorporation as a primitive corporal fantasy. If we return to Kristeva's idea of the introjection of the archaic object, it would be more adequate to refer to it as an incorporation taking place in an oral mode. The child swallows and devours what is perceived as pleasurable and expels what is felt as unpleasurable. Thus, introjection consists in a work of representation and symbolization with respect to the maternal body, in opposition to incorporation, which corresponds to a corporal fantasy taking place earlier. In this sense, incorporation constitutes the matrix of introjection.

From bodily fusion to differentiation

Due to the quality of 'sameness', the little girl's introjection of the object takes place in a much more immediate way than in the boy and this renders her prone to the mother's unconscious fantasies as well as her depressive feelings. The little girl has to tear herself from a relation that captures her and threatens her in terms of indifferentiation. In *Soleil noir*, Kristeva (1987) underlies the colossal effort that the girl has to make to detach herself from the mother in order to gain access to the symbolic as well as to sexuality, more particularly to sexuality with a partner of the opposite sex. Or, the little boy's relation to the mother implies necessarily the presence of an object sexually different from her. For the girl, differentiation requires the treatment of sexual excitation, which is introduced through the erotogenic zones such as the mouth, the anus and the vagina, during the corporal exchanges with the mother. The little girl faces the necessity to transform the excited cavity into a representation: 'the excited *cavity* of the interior of the body is transformed into an internal *representation*' (my own translation, original emphasis) (Kristeva, 2005, p. 232). Melanie Klein had already pointed to the young child's investment of the maternal body as having an interior, a hollow space. This mode of investment results in its symbolization in the form of a *psychic depth* that the girl has to appropriate. Hence, the girl's body image is constituted through the perception of the mother's body as a cavity that also contains the genitals. However, the girl's appropriation of her body as having an interior depends on the mother's relation to her own body. In the wake of puberty, the maternal body can become the source of an intense anxiety when the girl cannot reflect herself in the mother's psychic mirror, constituted not only by her face (Winnicott, 1971), but also by her body. The possibility of investing the mother's body acquires a particular value at this stage, leading to the consolidation of feminine identifications, which have already been established during childhood. For Zeynep, a young adolescent, the interior of her mother's body was impossible to fantasize as it was erected as an impenetrable, rigid wall. The mother's relation with her interior was phobic. Primitive emotions, such as hate of her own mother and incestuous fantasies in regard to her father, had to be split. The girl can identify with her mother's feminine qualities with the condition that the mother is not phobic with respect to her inner objects and can invest her own body and genitals as narcissistically valuable. The mother's capability to be vulnerable and be affected by the others allows the daughter to identify herself with a receptive body that has an interior and is soft. But Zeynep could not fantasize the interior of her mother's body. In this sense, the capability to receive and internalize is a feminine quality in both sexes, depending on the mother's introjective qualities. Zeynep's mother could not invest her daughter as having the same sex with her because she repudiated her own femininity, whereas she was seductive with her son, to whom she felt very close. Zeynep, who had difficulty in identifying herself with the phallic mother, projected herself as being neither feminine nor masculine. In other words, she situated herself as being neutral (Green, 1973). In fact, Zeynep's puberty had awakened the mother's infantile sexuality, as well as early processes related to separation. The daughter's puberty awakens the mother's incestual fantasies, but can also provoke early separation anxieties referring to the time when she was a baby (Bernateau, 2010). In this sense, the daughter's process of separation depends on the mother's differentiation from her own mother, reminding us that this process always concerns at least three generations of women.

Ms Fatma

Ms Fatma's problematic demonstrates that a woman's principal psychic work rests on separation and differentiation from the mother. Her somatic complaints were a mimetic reproduction of those suffered by the mother, as if the two bodies were in fusion or one inside the other. She identified with her mother's somatic complaints and symptoms in order to avoid separation; but separation required the elaboration of the incestuous fantasies with respect to the father as well as her rivalry with the mother. At this stage of the analytic work, she preferred to maintain the belief that she could not compete with her mother, whose femininity was enigmatic. This situation reminds us of the question: How does one become a woman and provoke a man's desire? Dora had confronted the same enigma, trying to resolve it by leaning on a female figure who was perceived as being feminine. Mrs K had served as an object of identification to Dora, whereas the woman analyst became the object of identification for Ms Fatma. At the beginning, it seemed to the patient that her mother's femininity was not something with which she could identify herself. Leaning on Lacan (1973), Marie-Magdeleine Lessana (2000) relates the traumatic relationship with the mother to the disappointment caused by the non-transmission of femininity. The non-transmission of femininity imprints the daughter's relation to the mother and this is precisely the cause of the violence and passion inherent in the love–hate relation between them.

Ms Fatma was about to get married. Separation from the mother provoked great upheaval and intense anxiety in her. The frequent illnesses that she suffered during this transition evoked the idea that her mother inhabited her body, impeding her from being with the lover and enjoying sexuality. She had a dream in which she had to leave her mother so that she and her husband could move to their new house. But before leaving, she had to tear off four of her fingers, which she did with considerable effort, and gave them to her mother. The dream created a certain perplexity in her as she could not confer any meaning to it. In fact, it signified that to love a man and experience sexual pleasure with him had a price. In order to separate from the mother and go to the lover, she had in return to offer four of her fingers to her. This compromise meant that she did not have to offer her entire being but only a part of her body. The underlying castration fantasy here is similar to that of a boy, who has to give up his penis with which he imagines that he satisfies his mother. In order not to lose his father's love, the boy has to renounce a partial object, his imaginary penis; whilst the girl's oedipal conflict concerns the threat of the loss of the mother, which represents the threat of losing her entire being, as the mother is the primary object but also the mirror of her being. Thanks to the act of castration in the dream, Ms Fatma succeeds in liberating herself from her mother, renouncing the *jouissance* of the fusion with her. Thus, the access to eroticism, that is to the erotic object, artistic and intellectual productions, has as a condition the *caesura* of the umbilical tie between mother and daughter.

In spite of being a talented designer of fashion, Ms Fatma felt frustrated in terms of her professional ambitions and considered that she was not creative enough in her work. A neurotic inhibition impeded her from realizing significant professional achievements. Each time she achieved significant progress, she found herself in a conflicted situation that served to detain her achievements and led to depressive feelings. Her professional achievements meant differentiation from the object. This situation represented a paradox to the extent that it was the mother who reclaimed her daughter's professional success. The mother had four daughters but my patient was the youngest and the elected one, to whom she had assigned the role of the child who would realize her dreams. Ms Fatma was envious of women and men who were professionally successful and with whom she competed. So, there was opposition between her envy and her feelings of self-mortification, an aspect that evokes Joan Riviere's female patient in 'Womanliness as a mascarade' (1929).

The display of the mascarade

Riviere's female patient was a very successful professional and intellectual. After fiercely competing with her male colleagues in her work, she needed to display a mascarade of womanliness, as she feared their reprisal. She became seductive with men and found herself in a self-sacrificing mode. Hence, her hysterical theatre aimed to transmit to her male colleagues the message that she did not possess the phallus and that she was a woman. Riviere underlines the inevitability of the masquerade when a woman aspires to professional achievements. Having been published in 1929, this paper referred to a society in which women's professional and intellectual aspirations were qualified as being masculine. What draws Riviere's attention is that the patient tried to conceal her penis-envy, which on the contrary tends to be overtly manifested. The patient's penis-envy can be situated in a social context in which the phallic aspirations of a woman were regarded as masculine and subject to prejudices. Some contemporary female analysts, such as Jacqueline Schaeffer (1997), consider that 'penis-envy' is an inevitable question in women's analysis and cannot be resolved. In this sense, she concurs with Freud (1937c), who attributes the resistance in analysis to penis-envy in women as well as to the fear of passivity in men. Susann Heenen-Wolff (2017), on her part, considers that gender discrimination is the cause of penis-envy, which is inevitable. However, we consider that penis-envy is a barrier that should be overcome in order to have access to the early conflicts and anxieties with respect to infantile objects, particularly with regard to the maternal object. Riviere focuses on the duality between her female patient's fierce competition with male colleagues and her recourse to the mascarade, which served to conceal her rivalry with them. And yet, her competition was not limited to her male colleagues, as she also manifested feelings of rivalry with regard to her parents. However, the conflict with respect to her parents is not examined in terms of the oedipal situation. Despite the absence of such a discussion, Riviere's (1929) paper is bright and, almost a hundred years later, her principal argument with respect to the duality between a woman's phallic aspirations and the 'mascarade' still keeps its validity.

This paper was written in homage to Ernest Jones's paper 'The early development of female sexuality' (1927). Riviere, who was a disciple of Melanie Klein, was evidently informed about both Klein's and Jones's approaches to the girl's early oedipal conflicts but she did not take these aspects into consideration. In this sense, we consider that the patient's mascarade served as a defensive protection against her conflicts with respect to the infantile objects. And yet, Riviere's discussion does not provide a reflexion on the unconscious motivations of her rivalry and aggression with respect to the parental objects. We have seen that the woman's early relation with the mother as well as her effort to detach herself is highly conflicted. Can we suppose that the competition with the father and her penis-envy served to conceal her conflicts with regard to the mother? Despite Riviere and Juranville (1993) conceiving recourse to the mascarade as typical in women, we consider, on the contrary, that it is necessary to go beyond what is displayed in order to penetrate the enigma presented by female sexuality. However, the use of the mascarade can sometimes be necessary when men feel threatened by women who can situate themselves in a desiring position and are successful. Lacan was interested by Riviere's clinical case because it illustrated the division that each woman experiences between the phallic functions and the female functions. He discussed it in his seminar *Les formations de l'inconscient* (1957–1958) in order to illustrate that female sexuality is necessarily conflicted by this division. The characteristics that Riviere's patient displayed, such as being a good housewife and having a satisfactory intimate life with the husband, seem to Lacan to reflect an apparently complete development in terms of femininity. He concurs with Riviere when he considers that the wearing of a mask is, properly speaking, feminine. We would like to emphasize two aspects in Lacan's approach. First, he does not differentiate between gender as a social construction and what would be constitutive of femininity. The patient's qualities underlined by him seem to reflect an 'almost complete development' in terms of femininity, whereas from our point of view they involve to a great extent a certain social construction of gender. Second, while Lacan attributes the source of the conflict to the division between a woman's feminine and phallic functions, he does not take into consideration her relation to the infantile objects, particularly to the mother.

The melancholic core

For the girl, the price of being herself consists in separation and mourning of the maternal object (Chabert, 2003). Each subject, be it a woman or a man, faces the challenge of separation from the maternal object. This issue should be considered with respect to 'the feminine of the psyche' (Cournut-Janin, 1999), which is constituted by means of primary identification and primary homosexuality. In some analysis of women, Cournut-Janin refers to the apparition, especially in the phase of termination, of a melancholic core. A sudden eruption of violent affects invades the analytic space, when analysis had till then taken place in the neurotic register. This imprevisible seismic change constitutes a bedrock that is opposed to the continuation and finalization of the analytic work. In the transference, the woman analyst finds she is the object of hate of her patient, who feels captured by an archaic maternal imago. To hate the object becomes a way of freeing herself from an invasive identification. Thus, a regression to an early organization of the ego takes place, to the time in which 'an ego hardly emerging struggles for existence' (my own translation) (Cournut-Janin, 1999, p. 58). The analyst and the patient find themselves struggling between life and death, a situation that is evocative of the reactivation of primary agonies (Winnicott, 1974). Jozef Perelberg describes in similar terms the analytic process with her patient Emma. The analyst is 'involved in a deadly battle, where one does not know whether the patient or the analyst will survive – a confusion between life and death' (2018, p. 115). Cournut-Janin examines the daughter's archaic maternal imago in relation with a mother who has not been able to separate from her own mother. The mother projects on her daughter the disappointment of not having been recognized in her own singularity and identity by her own mother and loved as such. Hence, the mother's ambivalent and passional imago of her own mother marks the relation to her daughter.

In her article 'From bisexuality to the feminine' (2018), Jacqueline Godfrind joins Cournut-Janin's findings with respect to the melancholic core and notes the presence of a bewitching maternal imago with respect to the daughter.

> Behind the sometimes deadly hate that exists between daughter and mother, suddenly there appears a bewildered love for the mother, a fascination that rivets the daughter to the mother, appealing to an encounter *'de trou à trou'* ('hole to hole'), the daughter being totally attached to the mother, bewitched, a link I call *'primary homosexuality'*.
> (Godfrind, 2018, p. 124, emphasis in original)

Her approach to this question in this text is more radical than her former conceptualization in her book, published seventeen years earlier. Whereas in the text of 2018 she considers that a melancholic core tends to characterize the relation between mother and daughter, in 2001 this problematic is limited to a pathological relation between them. She names the excessive perturbation of the daughter's tie to the mother as a 'black pact' sealed between the two and she situates its origin in the context of the mother's conflicted relation to her baby daughter. In a normal process, the girl identifies with the mother, who invests her baby daughter and imprints her unconscious fantasies to her. It is to the mother's early imprinting that Godfrind attributes the transmission of the matrix of femininity. We consider that each daughter's femininity is inevitably marked by symptoms that link her to the mother's history and refers to at least three generations. The price of being the daughter of that particular mother passes through the imperative of elaborating the conflicts transmitted by her, particularly when femininity is at stake. The conflicts to be symbolized are related to the mother's narcissistic injuries. In fact, it becomes the daughter's debt to the mother to elaborate and appropriate them. Godfrind emphasizes to what degree the 'black pact' impedes the possibility of being autonomous, to access the erotic object as well as maternity and cultural development. Hence, the 'black pact' with the mother signs conflicts of a narcissistic nature that are related to the impossibility of renouncing the object of prehistory, a period beyond memory. At this point, Cournut-Janin speaks of the abolition of generational differences. However, the Oedipus complex belongs to the realm of what can be organized and symbolized in the form of a history, in which sexual difference and generational difference have been established. What draws Godfrind's attention are the impediments to the satisfactory development of the girl's femininity, specially when the mother's representation of it corresponds to feelings of shame and malediction provoked by her relation to her own mother. I will discuss Ms Aisha's analytic process, which serves to illustrate the 'black version of the feminine' (Cournut-Janin, 1999).

Ms Aisha

Ms Aisha's demand for analysis had taken place shortly after having terminated psychotherapy with a male therapist. Our first interview was marked by a long silence and it would be more appropriate to speak of a blank in terms of the absence of any possible expression of affects and words. A few months later, in one of the sessions she communicated to me that a part of herself was like a blank sheet of paper. The aspect of blankness here was not due to the repression of memories in a neurotic sense but to the presence of traumatic forces that could not be represented and symbolized. However, in this first interview we were able to transform the void into a space of words, thoughts and affects and she could speak to me about the loss of her father, killed in a car accident, when she was a young child. The finalization of the psychotherapy, hence the separation from her male therapist, had awakened the traumatic experience of her father's death, which had been silenced in her since her childhood. Hence, our work had allowed her to establish a link between the recent separation from her therapist and the loss of her father. She had solicited the second interview two months later and with a sense of urgency. She was pregnant and her husband was opposed to her wish to have a child.

'I want this child' she said and cried. This conception, which had taken place after the first interview, had been the fruit of the analytic encounter. The latter had allowed her to talk about her father's traumatic loss and express her affects with respect to it. The analytic encounter had, at the same time, awakened her libido, showing the effects of the woman analyst's body on the woman patient's psyche. In this sense, it had been significant that the encounter was realized by a woman analyst. The demand for analysis corresponded not only to the necessity to work through the traumatic loss of the father, but more importantly, it concerned the need to work through the traumatic relationship with the mother and elaborate on the feminine. The feminine and maternal qualities of the analyst were symbolized in the transference by the warmth of the intimacy, as well as by the smell of the food that she had perceived coming from the kitchen. However, Ms Aisha's pregnancy produced an upheaval that converted analysis into a tortuous experience characterized by the surge of explosive affects. In fact, this affective intensity was the opposite of the state of psychic death in which she used to live and with which she had presented herself to the first interview. The analytic sessions soon became the theatre of obsessive and torturing ideas with respect to the health and integrity of the baby. She could not continue her pregnancy which she seemed to long for. Despite a positive transference that she had established with me, she began to feel persecuted. She was tormented by the idea that the baby inside her could develop abnormally and that it was too dangerous for her to keep it. She could not continue her pregnancy and invest in the baby, without being invaded by the hallucination of the 'dead mother'. The shade of the object that had fallen on the ego was projected onto the analytic scene. Her pregnancy reactivated the 'dead mother' imago, which converted the interior of her body into a dead and black place. An extreme state of agitation beyond words and representations seized her and she feared being annihilated. In *Life narcissism, death narcissism* (2001), André Green refers to the concept of 'the dead mother', which consists in an *imago* that has been constituted in the young child as a result of maternal depression. The object, which was lively till then, suddenly loses its vitality and becomes aloof. Hence, the mother is transformed into a person psychically dead, whose face becomes strange and can no more reflect the child's affects and in this sense is terrorizing. This imago invades the child's psychic space, provoking a perturbation with respect to the libidinal investment of the objects, including that of the maternal object. A severe and radical disinvestment leaves traces in the psyche in the form of 'holes' that the subject fills with his or her destructive impulses. Green remarks that the patient's destructivity is the result of the weakening of the libidinal investment, caused by the severe disinvestment of the maternal object.

Ms Aisha's crisis provoked the explosion of something that had irrupted into the analytic scene, as it was unnameable and irrepresentable. The baby became a persecuting internal object that had to be eliminated. Something strange occurred in the third session that I would only realize in the next session. In the fourth session, she communicated to me that I had ended the anterior session fifteen minutes earlier. She did not come to the following session. She attended the sixth session, announcing to me that she had aborted on the day that she had not attended the session.

P: I felt relieved, I cried a lot and I expelled it.
A: I expelled you also, allowing you to leave the session fifteen minutes earlier.

By ending the third session fifteen minutes earlier, I had given her the possibility of liberating herself from a persecuting maternal imago. By means of my enactment, I had helped her to get rid of the baby. Despite her desire for the baby, she had found it was impossible to continue her pregnancy, due to her fear of punishment by the envious and fierce maternal imago. Her mother envied all that her daughter possessed: a husband, babies and economic prosperity. In this sense, the baby that she carried in her body had to be offered as a sacrifice to the ferocious maternal imago. However, her feelings of guilt were ultimately related to the conception of the baby as being the fruit of incest. The conception of the child, which had marked the beginning of our analytic work, had been the fruit of sexual pleasure with her husband, as she would verbalize later. Hence, the interruption of her pregnancy seemed necessary in order to avoid a catastrophe. The continuation of her pregnancy would mean that she was capable of liberating herself from the ferocious maternal imago and move to the husband (father). The possibility of having been capable of signifying her father's tragic loss during the first interview had allowed her to give a place to her husband as an erotic object and enjoy sex with him. This sudden change at the very beginning of analysis, which *convulsed* her psychic economy, was the effect of a positive transference. The analyst was perceived as seductive to the degree that she represented a lively feminine object. However, the awakening of her libido had taken place too soon and she did not have the necessary psychic equipment for it. She needed to continue to exist as a living dead for a long time. She feared that the continuation of her pregnancy could bring about something catastrophic, that of the loss of her daughter. In fact, she already had a girl. The insatiable maternal super-ego could retaliate for having been abandoned by her daughter. The birth of the baby would mean that she had chosen the husband (father) and not the mother. Thus, there was no possibility for triangulation and what was at stake was the foreclosure (Lacan, 1957–1958) of the symbolic father. On the other hand, could she authorize herself to have a baby when her mother, due to her age, could not procreate anymore?

The 'dead mother' that Ms Aisha encountered as a baby could not dream but could only survive the traumatic losses that she had undergone as a young woman. The latter had experienced successive losses of her parents and other close figures. The mother's psychic reality consisted in a bi-dimensional universe (Bick, 1968; Tustin, 1995; Meltzer et al., 1975) characterized by the necessity to project and expulse. She managed to survive the traumatic losses by expelling all affects and thoughts that were painful and acted according to her raw instincts. The mother revolted against the destiny that had mercilessly struck her. Her laughter was diabolical, but so was her destiny. The mother was perceived as being intrusive due to the sexual excitation that she aroused in her daughter and this situation provoked revulsion and rage in my patient. The sexual disgust that she felt in those moments corresponded to something abject, which became an attempt to distance herself from her mother's body. The expulsion of the affects by the mother converted her into a person without memory and this situation provoked a void in the patient's psychic reality that impeded her from relating to the anterior generations and inserting herself in a maternal lineage. The generational rupture suffered by Ms Aisha put, on the other hand, her pubescent daughter in psychic danger.

In fact, the beginning of her analysis had coincided with her daughter's awakening to puberty and this event had converted the analytic scene into the theatre of wild sexual impulses. Ms Aisha's pubescent sexuality, awakened by that of her daughter, seemed to lack a human signification as if it were something animal and mad. She was incapable of having an insight into her daughter's psyche. She could not elaborate and transform the wild excitations aroused by her daughter's body and felt invaded by them. She tried to surmount these chaotic moments by denying separation and clung to her daughter. On one occasion, she said: 'I have stuck to her with so much passion. I want her to be identical to me'. The sexual violence that she projected onto her daughter entailed strong feelings of guilt and provoked intense counter-transferential feelings in me. At those moments, maintaining my neutrality became very hard. She feared her own destructivity with respect to her daughter. On the other hand, she could not tolerate her daughter's liveliness when she herself felt like a living dead. Ms Aisha's need to be identical to her daughter reflected the primitive need to merge with her, a need that represents a major threat with respect to differentiation. Françoise Héritier, a French anthropologist, states that 'the prohibition of incest protects from the horror of the identical' (2001, p. 98, my own translation). She calls the incestual tie between mother and daughter or between two sisters 'fundamental incest' to the extent that it reproduces the identical. The incestual tie between two women represents a major threat to differentiation, whereas the incestual tie between two men would not be as threatening as each of them has been procreated by a woman.

Several years of analysis had gone by. A sudden and unexpected change occurred when Ms Aisha decided to divorce her husband. It was an act that corresponded to a kind of psychic dissolution, a 'dismantlement' (Meltzer et al., 1975) that took place silently and without any mourning. It was difficult to explain it because the auto-destruction had taken place at a time when she had accomplished notable progress in her analysis. After having gone through numerous breakdowns, upheavals and convulsions, her psychic world had attained a certain integration and stabilization. Divorcing her husband meant that she was renouncing the possibility of an erotic life with a man. Hence, she sacrificed her erotic love life with her husband in exchange for her liberation from the vampiric maternal imago. She could only authorize herself the pleasure that she took from intellectual and spiritual activities as well as from her professional life. When she began analysis she was moderately religious. Later, she belonged to an Islamic group that studied and discussed the fundamental texts of the religion. The religious reference was important because it intervened as a third party that supported and sustained her. The symbolic father representing the prohibition of incest was foreclosed and did not operate in her psychic reality. In this sense, belonging to the religious group provided a sense of identity without awakening sexual excitation in her and also became her way of resolving her attachment to me. Her engagement in the group signed the beginning of her detachment from me till the day she abruptly announced to me that she wished to end her analysis. 'I have used your presence and the work here for healing myself and now that I feel well, I am leaving you'. By these words, she was referring to the matricidal act characterizing separation. Belonging to a female group provided her a sense of identity and sublimation became the solution she found to her sexual drives.

The melancholic process and the impossibility of conceiving a child

Ms Aisha's unbearable state of anxiety had led to the compulsion to get rid of the baby, as her pregnancy had dangerously confronted her to the insatiable and persecuting maternal imago. Despite André Green (1983) situating the constitution of the imago of 'the dead mother' in the months following birth, we consider that the mother's depression can also take place during pregnancy and affect the symbiotic union between her and the foetus. However, the constitution of the imago of 'the dead mother' in the child requires a certain psychic development that can only be attained during the first months of life. Cournut-Janin (1999) adds a new aspect to the discussion of 'the dead mother', by referring to another kind of narcissistic loss. The latter is constituted in the relation of the baby daughter to the mother, who has not been able to detach herself from her own mother and has been disappointed, as she was not recognized and loved as a girl. Hence, the daughter is captured by the mother's conflicted primary homosexuality, which consists in a fixation on her own mother. This fixation signifies that the mother has not been able to differentiate herself from her own mother and make an object–change towards the father. This situation leads to the abolition of generational differences between the daughter, the mother and the grandmother. We consider that the mother's disappointment, due to her own mother's lack of recognition and love, has a weight on her daughter's narcissism. Here, a narcissistic injury has taken place before the constitution of the ego and for this reason it has to be distinguished from frustration. The latter supposes that the ego has already been constituted and that the subject has been differentiated from the object. In this perspective, frustration is relative to the impediment of a libidinal satisfaction with respect to the object. Sylvie Faure-Pragier (1999) remarks that the daughter's fixation on the maternal object can in some cases provoke infertility. She concurs with Cournut-Janin when she speaks of a mother who has not been able to please her own mother for having been born as a girl. She finds that at least three generations of women are concerned in the resulting infertility of the daughter. The fixation of the mother on her own mother would be the result of a conflicted primary homosexuality that excludes the identification with the father both as a symbolic and libidinal object. The impossibility of identifying with the paternal object ensues from a mother who has not desired the father and who is fixated on her own mother. In the transference, the woman analyst's body provides a container, but also a mirror allowing the edification of primary homosexuality.

In another patient, Ms Leila, the transformations in analysis brought about an important opening in her psychic life, along with the capacity to establish affective ties with others. Then came a period in which she wished to become a mother. Some of her dreams were an attempt to realize the presence of a good and tender mother, in whose protection she could get pregnant. She needed to conceive the baby first in her mind in order to have a representation of it inside her body. Such a representation can only be constituted when the little girl can libidinally invest the interior of the mother's body and introject her maternal qualities. However, Ms Leila could not fantasize the interior of her mother's body as a nurturing space in which a baby could develop and grow. In the transference, the elaboration of what was inside her own body passed by the possibility of fantasizing the analyst as a container that would not imprison her in a claustrophobic sense and this meant a certain circulation of affects in the analytic work. In one of her dreams she was in an archaeological site and had entered a building that had several entries and exits. This was a configuration of her body with the erotogenic orifices – the entries and the exits – open to the outside world, in exchange with the objects. The dream represented a lively and erotic body that occupied an extension (Coblence, 2010) in the world, as was the image of the archaeological site. Freud had put in 'Findings, ideas, problems' the following note: 'Space may be the projection of the extension of the psychical apparatus' (1941f, p. 300). Space becomes the projection of the extension of the psyche to the extent that the process of symbolization allows openings towards the external world, along with the possibility of using the objects. However, a significant change occurred when Ms Leila became pregnant. Tortuous affects, like in Ms Aisha's case, invaded the analytic scene, along with the eruption of a persecuting maternal imago. We cannot say that a melancholic core had emerged unexpectedly, as was the case with Cournut-Janin's (1999) or Jozef Perelberg's (2018) female patients. But we had never experienced till then such a dark period in which she struggled between life and death. Her pregnancy reactivated 'the dead mother' imago, which converted the interior of her body into a dead and black place. An extreme state of agitation beyond words and representations seized Ms Leila and she feared being annihilated. In the case of another patient, Ms Alina, the threatening maternal imago had led to the impossibility of introjecting the object's maternal qualities. She experienced her own body as a bi-dimensional space, without depth and as strong and cold as steel. Her body had to be as strong as steel so that it could not be penetrated by the persecuting maternal imago. In this sense, the transformation of the body from a bi-dimensional space to a three-dimensional space that includes qualities of warmth, depth and sensuality, requires crossing a long way in analysis as well as elaborating the envious attacks directed at the woman analyst. The latter is perceived as possessing not only maternal and feminine qualities but also other riches with respect to cultural and intellectual objects. As in the case of Ms Alina, transformations in the analytic process gave way to the presence of a lively, warm and nourishing internal space, a uterus, in which not only a human baby but other sublimatory creations could come into existence.

Reflecting on the feminine and the melancholic, Catherine Chabert (2003) observes in some women's analysis a defect of the hysterical construction of the fantasy of seduction, that is the fantasy of being beaten by the father, and instead finds a melancholic version of it. In the hysterical version, the fantasy of being beaten by the father acquires the signification of the coital act, is repressed during the resolution of the Oedipus complex and can only be revealed by analysis. In the melancholic version of the fantasy of seduction, Chabert underlies a defect in terms of the repression of the beating-fantasy that gives way to a real scene in which the girl has the conviction that she has seduced the father. Or, by assuring a passive representation of the scene, the hysterical version of the fantasy of seduction protects the girl from an excess of excitation that is disorganizing. In the hysterical version, it is the father who becomes the seducer to whom excitation is attributed. This representation, notes Chabert, allows the sexual drive to undergo a reversal from activity to passivity, reversal that would not operate in the melancholic version. The conviction of having seduced the father would provoke the extinction of the libido, hence that of the investment of the objects. Until her encounter with the woman analyst, Ms Aisha's existence evoked that of a living dead. However, the awakening of the libido that had led to her pregnancy had become very dangerous. She felt threatened by the ferocious maternal imago for having enjoyed sexuality with her husband (father). The baby as the fruit of incest had to be eliminated. The awakening of her libido felt threatening from the beginning till the end of analysis and led her to resort to a radical solution, that of eliminating her femininity and sexual life. In our experience with Ms Leila, Ms Alina and other women patients, the wish to get pregnant could not be realized to the extent that it concerned incestuous fantasies with respect to the father. Coitus with the lover signified the incestuous union with the father in a *real* sense, that is without having undergone symbolization and repression. This reminds us of the observation that Lacan makes with respect to the young homosexual's wish to have a child by the father. It was not on an *imaginary* level but in a *real* sense that the young girl had experienced her wish and this aspect seemed preoccupying to Lacan. The young girl's disappointment with respect to having a child by the father at the moment when the mother had had a boy by the father, had led to the repudiation of her femininity. We know that Lacan conceives the psychic structure in terms of the registers of the *imaginary*, the *symbolic* and the *real*. It is the symbolic register that protects the subject against the intrusion of the real in the form of hallucination and operates via the internalization of castration and the paternal metaphor (Chemama & Vandermersch, 2003). In other words, the wish of the young homosexual to have a child or the desire for pregnancy of some of my women patients did not concern an unconscious fantasy related to it. However, the unconscious fantasy supposes the existence of repression and this particularity is, according to Laplanche (1997), what constitutes sexuality and protects the subject from the threat of incestuous wishes.

References

Abraham, K. (1924). Esquisse d'une histoire du développement de la libido basée sur la psychanalyse des troubles mentaux. *Développement de la libido. Oeuvres complètes* – 2. Paris: Payot, 1966.

Bernateau, I. (2010). *L'adolescent et la séparation*. Paris: PUF.

Bick, E. (1968). The experience of the skin in early object–relations. *International journal of psychoanalysis, 49*: 484–486.

Chabert, C. (2003). *Féminin mélancolique*. Paris: PUF.

Chemama, R. & Vandermersch, B. (2003). *Dictionnaire de la psychanalyse*. Paris: Larousse.

Coblence, F. (2010). La vie d'âme. Psyché est corporelle, n'en sait rien. *Revue française de psychanalyse*, 5, 1285–1356.

Cournut-Janin, M. (1998). *Féminin et féminité*. Paris: PUF.

Cournut-Janin, M. (1999). Le noyau mélancolique, féminin, tel qu'il se découvre dans l'analyse, et le plus souvent au décours d'une cure, voire d'une tranche. In: J. Schaeffer, M. Cournut-Janin, S. Faure-Pragier & F. Guignard (Eds.), *Clés pour le féminin*. Paris: PUF.

Cournut-Janin, M. (2015). The same and the other: homosexuality in adolescence. In: E. Abrevaya & F. Thomson-Salo (Eds.), *Homosexualities*. London: Karnac.

Denis, P. (2005). Homosexualité primaire, base de contradiction. *Revue française de psychanalyse*, 46:1, 35–42.

Denis, P. (2005). Narcisse indifférent. In: J. André (Ed.), *Les sexes indifférents*. Paris: PUF.

Denis, P. (2015). Gender as heritage of the first qualitative differentiation. In: E. Abrevaya & F. Thomson-Salo (Eds.), *Homosexualities*. London: Karnac.

Faure-Pragier, S. (1999). Le désir d'enfant comme substitut du penis manquant: Une théorie stérile de la féminité. In: J. Schaeffer, M. Cournut-Janin, S. Faure-Pragier & F. Guignard (Eds.), *Clés pour le féminin*. Paris: PUF.

Ferenczi, S. (1909). Transfert et introjection. *Psychanalyse 1. Oeuvres complètes*. Paris: Payot, 1982.

Ferenczi, S. (1912). Le concept d'introjection. *Psychanalyse 1. Oeuvres complètes*. Paris: Payot, 1982.

Freud, S. (1915c). Instincts and their vicissitudes. *SE*, 14: 111–140.

Freud, S. (1917e). Mourning and melancholia. *SE*, 14: 239–258.

Freud, S. (1919e). A child is being beaten. *SE*, 17: 179–204.

Freud, S. (1923a). *The ego and the id. SE*, 19: 3–66.

Freud, S. (1937c). Analysis terminable and interminable. *SE*, 23: 211–253.

Freud, S. (1941f). Findings, ideas, problems. *SE*, 23: 299–300.

Godfrind, J. (2001). *Comment la féminité vient aux femmes*. Paris: PUF.

Godfrind, J. (2018). From bisexuality to the feminine. In: R. Jozef Perelberg (Ed.), *Psychic bisexuality*. London: Routledge.

Green, A. (1973). Le genre neutre. In: J.-B. Pontalis (Ed.), *Bisexualité et différence de sexes*. Paris: Gallimard.

Green, A. (1983). Le complexe de la mère morte. *Narcissisme de vie, narcissisme de mort*. Paris: Minuit.

Green, A. (2001). *Life narcissism, death narcissism*. London: Free Association Books.

Heenen-Wolff, S. (2017). *Contre la normativité en psychanalyse*. Paris: Editions in Press.

Héritier, F. (2001). Inceste et substance. Oedipe, Allen, les autres et nous. In: J. André (Ed.), *Incestes*. Paris: PUF.

Jones, E. (1927). The early development of female sexuality. *International journal of psychoanalysis*, 5, 50–65.

Juranville, A. (1993). *La femme et la mélancolie*. Paris: PUF.

Kestemberg, E. (1984). Astrid ou homosexualité, identité, adolescence. Quelques propositions hypothétiques. *Les cahiers du Centre de Psychanalyse et de Psychothérapie*, no. 8.

Klein, M. (1930). The importance of symbol-formation in the development of the ego. *International journal of psycho-analysis*, 11, 24–39.

Klein, M. (1932). *Psycho-analysis of children*. London: Hogarth.

Kristeva, J. (1987). *Soleil noir. Dépression et mélancolie*. Paris: Gallimard.

Kristeva, J. (1992). *Black sun. Depression and melancholia*. New York: Columbia University Press.

Kristeva, J. (2005). La fatigue au féminin. *La haine et le pardon*. Paris: Fayard.

Lacan, J. (1953–1954). *Séminaire. Livre I. Les écrits techniques de Freud*. Paris: Seuil, 1975.

Lacan, J. (1957–1958). *Séminaire. Livre V. Les formations de l'inconscient*. Paris: Seuil, 1998.

Lacan, J. (1964). *Séminaire. Livre XI. Les quatre concepts fondamentaux de la psychanalyse*. Paris: Seuil, 1973.

Lacan, J. (1973). *L'étourdit. Scilicet*, 4, 5–52.

Laplanche, J. (1997). *Le primat de l'autre en psychanalyse*. Paris: Flammarion.

Laplanche, J. & Pontalis, J.-B. (1988). *The language of psychoanalysis*. London: Routledge.

Lessana, M.-M. (2000). *Entre mère et fille: Un ravage*. Paris: Fayard.

Meltzer, D., Bremner, J., Hoxter, S., Weddell, D., & Wittenberg, I. (Eds.) (1975). *Explorations in autism*. London: Harris Meltzer Trust.

Perelberg, R. Jozef (2018). Love and melancholia in the analysis of women. In: R. Jozef Perelberg (Ed.), *Psychic bisexuality*. London: Routledge.

Riviere, J. (1929). Womanliness as a mascarade. *International journal of psycho-analysis*, 10, 303–313.

Schaeffer, J. (1997). *Le refus du féminin*. Paris: PUF.

Segal, H. (1974). *Introduction to the work of Melanie Klein*. New York: Basic Books.

Torok, M. (1987). Maladie du deuil et fantasme du cadavre exquis. In: N. Abraham & M. Torok. *L'écorce et le noyau*. Paris: Flammarion.

Tustin, F. (1995). *Autism and childhood psychosis*. London: Routledge.

Winnicott, D.W. (1971). Mirror-role of mother and family in child development. *Playing and reality*. London: Tavistock Publications.

Winnicott, D.W. (1974). Fear of breakdown. *International review of psycho-analysis*, 1, 103–107.

5   Gender, the sexual and the feminine

The masculine and the feminine

In 2003, Jean Laplanche publishes an important essay on gender in the context of French psychoanalysis. This work would later figure as part of a collection of essays in *Sexual* (2007) and translated into English as *Freud and the sexual* (2011). Laplanche notes that the word 'gender' is missing in Freud's work in spite of his reflexion on three opposite couples: 'active–passive', 'phallic–castrated' and 'masculine–feminine'. Freud's first reflexion on masculine–feminine appears in a note added in 1915 to *Three essays* (1905d) and his reflexion gets richer thanks to his papers 'Female sexuality' (1931b) and 'Femininity' (1933a). In the latter, he remarks: 'When you meet a human being, the first distinction you make is "male or female?" and you are accustomed to make the distinction with unhesitating certainty' (1933a, p. 113). However, despite the clear anatomical distinction between male and female, it is not possible to give a definite explanation of masculinity and femininity. In spite of the sociological and cultural factors that establish a correspondence between masculinity and activity, from the viewpoint of psychoanalysis it would be inadequate to consider the fact that masculine behaviour coincides with activity and feminine behaviour with passivity.

> One might consider characterizing femininity psychologically as giving preference to passive aims. This is not, of course the same thing as passivity; to achieve a passive aim may call for a large amount of activity. A mother is active in every sense towards her child; the act of lactation itself may equally be described as the mother suckling the baby or as being sucked by it.
>
> (1933a, p. 115)

It is possible to establish an analogy between the mother and the analyst, who both have to realize a significant amount of activity to obtain a receptive position. The analyst's receptivity consists in being open to the patient's most primitive affects, such as love and hate, greed, envy and aggression,

DOI: 10.4324/9781003232261-5

and corresponds to their transformation by means of his or her *reverie*. Hence, the product of the analyst's work becomes a psychic nourishment.

Leaning on the works of American psychoanalysts, such as Stoller (1964, 1994), Roiphe and Galenson (1981), Laplanche affirms that gender identity is established as early as the period of fifteen months. He acknowledges the contributions made by gender studies, particularly by Judith Butler (1990, 1993) and enters into a dialogue with her by introducing the term gender into French psychoanalysis as early as 1980. In *Castration. Symbolisations* (1980) he remarks in a note: There is 'a recognition of the *distinction of genders preceding the difference of sexes*' (Laplanche, 1980, p. 33, my own translation, emphasis in original). Here, his position is close to Stoller (1964, 1994). However, contrary to Stoller, Laplanche takes the measure of differentiating gender and sex, as the first tends to be reduced to psychological factors and the second to anatomical elements. Christophe Dejours (2003) differentiates between gender and sex, an aspect that tends to be neglected by those who work in the field of gender studies. By 'gender', Dejours refers to the behaviour and fantasies related to the distinction masculine–feminine, whereas by 'sex' he conceives the behaviour and fantasies related to the sexuated function and sexual pleasure. Due to the denaturalized dimension of human sexuality and the hierarchical position of heterosexuality marked by male domination, André notes that 'psychoanalysis finds itself on the same ground with *gender studies*' (André, 2017, p. 33, my own translation, emphasis in original). The sexual drive characterizes the denaturalized aspect of human sexuality to the extent that it is a deviation from the instinct and is always associated with the unconscious fantasy. In the absence of a regulation of the sexual instinct, it is society, the *socius*, that takes over the function of regulating sexuality. At this point both psychoanalysis and gender studies share a common ground. However, there is a point of divergence between them as psychoanalysis conceives psychic phenomena through the prism of the unconscious. Judith Butler and others find support for their arguments against heterosexuality in Freud's interrogation on this matter. In *Three essays* (1905d), in a note added in 1915, Freud states:

> On the contrary, psychoanalysis considers that a choice of an object independently of its sex – freedom to range equally over male and female objects – as it is found in childhood, in primitive states of society and early periods of history, is the original basis from which, as a result of restriction in one direction or the other, both the normal and inverted develop.
>
> (1905d, p. 146)

However, as André puts it, Freud's approach on this matter does not mean that the subject has the freedom to choose his/her gender, nor to make a 'natural' object–choice, as psychic reality is greatly determined by the unconscious. On the other hand, polymorphic perversity, which is one of the characteristics of infantile sexuality, does not consist in the freedom to multiply the sexes. Even if it were possible to imagine, remarks Jean-Michel Lévy (2019), the free exercise of polymorphy as well as liberation with respect to gender and identity, is never exempt from conflict and anxiety. Psychoanalysis has demonstrated the conflicted nature of psychic reality, divided between the exigencies of the *socius* and the excitation arising in the body and defying 'the primacy of the genital'.

The triad: gender, sex and the *sexual*

Laplanche studies the couple masculine–feminine by means of a triad: gender, sex and the *sexual*. These three elements are constitutive of sexuality but also characterized by their distinctiveness. Gender is assigned to the child by the other, the *socius*, which corresponds to parents, relatives, but also to influential figures in the family. These parental and familiar figures 'bombard' the child with their preconscious–conscious messages, which are messages of assignment of gender. Among the enigmatic messages that are conveyed, those that have a major impact on the child emanate from the adult's unconscious sexual fantasies. In fact, the latter convey 'noises' belonging to the sphere of the *sexual*. By using a neologism such as the *sexual*, Laplanche refers to the parents' repressed infantile sexuality, reactivated by the perception of the child's body. The newborn's body triggers the parents' unconscious sexual fantasies. Hence, under the effect of such fantasies, the parents attribute 'the sex of a fantasized anatomy' (Laplanche, 2007) to their child, independently of the anatomical sex. The messages conveyed to the child consist of a set of complex acts that are continuous and have a prescriptive character. On this point, Laplanche and Butler concur with respect to the weight of the *socius* in the assignment of gender. In this sense, gender is the result of the identification of the child *by* the adult and not the inverse, that is the identification *with* the adult. Butler considers that the construction of sex is not a causal process that can be initiated by a subject. 'Construction not only takes place *in* time, but itself is a temporal process which operates through the reiteration of norms; sex is both produced and destabilized in the course of this reiteration' (Butler, 1993, p. 10). Despite that both authors agree on the impact of reiteration underlying the construction of gender, their divergence, however, is significant. For Butler, reiteration refers to the continuous action of social norms, whereas for Laplanche it concerns the continuous effect of the adult's preconscious and unconscious messages on the child. André Green (1973) remarks that the attribution of gender to the child depends very closely on the parental desire, which has an effect of impregnation. By emphasizing the impact of social determinism, Butler (1993) leaves out the effects of the adult's unconscious sexual fantasies on the child. Dejours (2003) emphasizes that this aspect is also ignored and neglected by other theoreticians of gender and society, who lean on the work of Michel Foucault in their reflexion on political philosophy and refer to Lacan, Derrida, Deleuze and Guattari in their conceptualization of sexuality.

The medical authority and the assignment of gender

Michel Foucault makes the discovery of a nineteenth-century text, *Herculine Barbin. Being the recently discovered memoirs of nineteenth century French hermaphrodite* (1980), which shows the impact of the assignment of gender by the *socius*. Herculine Barbin, named Alexina, was raised in a convent and later in a boarding school for young girls till the age of twenty-two. In this sense, she was raised as a girl. The medical authorities considered that an error had been committed in the assignment of Alexina's gender at birth and that it was necessary to correct it, aiming at establishing the 'true sex' (Foucault, 1980). At the age of twenty-two, her civil state was re-formed and a reassignment was realized by the jurisdiction. Hence, Alexina had to become a man and take the name of Abel. Her memoirs give an account of the tragic effects of this reassignment of her gender, leading her to commit suicide at the age of thirty. Alexina had written her memoirs feeling as a woman till her entry into the universe of men, from which she felt totally excluded. In this sense, what strikes the reader of the *Memoirs* is the confusion of not knowing how to designate its author. The change of enunciation in the text from the feminine to the masculine or vice versa 'destabilizes the language' (Laufer, 2010) and cancels its function of differentiation and identification. After the reassignment of her gender, Alexina/Abel had to quit the region in which she was raised and in which she worked and move to Paris. The total isolation along with the material and psychological misery in which Alexina/Abel found herself/himself were devastating and precipitated her tragic end. In opposition to the medical authorities' scientific scrutiny of which Alexina had been the object, the religious authorities in the nineteenth century were free from the conception of establishing 'the true sex'. The reassignment of gender by the medical authorities had had ravaging effects on Alexina/Abel, whereas there had been no necessity for the definition of her gender in the convent where she was raised. In the convent she could live in the ambiguity of her gender. In this sense, the reassignment of Alexina's gender by the medical authorities serves to illustrate its prescriptive nature which refers to a knowledge of the 'sex' beyond what the individual can know or choose about himself or herself.

The reception of the enigmatic messages by the child

Laplanche (2007) is particularly concerned by the way gender is *received and appropriated by the child* and does not agree with the idea of the passivity with which it is internalized, as defended by the sociologists and theorists of gender. On the contrary, the child has to realize a psychic work in order to appropriate the messages that are 'implanted' into the psyche in the encounter with the adult, who has a sexual life, more particularly unconscious sexual fantasies. Laplanche names this asymmetry the 'fundamental anthropological situation', which is epitomized by Ferenczi's (1932) paper on the 'confusion of tongues' between the child and the adult. The 'fundamental anthropological situation' refers to the encounter between an immature child who is completely dependent on the adult's care and attention and an adult who has a mature sexuality, and in this sense there is no possible symmetry between them. The child has sexual drives but the access to sexual representations and the realization of the sexual act are only possible at puberty. In *Life and death in psychoanalysis* (1985), Laplanche remarks that the erotogenic zones of the young child are zones of exchange with the mother while she imparts her care and attention. Parental fantasies, particularly those of the mother, focus on these zones, through which is introduced sexual excitation. In other words, sexuality comes to the child from the other and its genesis is not due to biology.

In *Essays on otherness* (1999), Laplanche underlines a major aspect: what is external at first becomes internalized thereafter. At the beginning, the adult's messages are intrusive as they generate excitation but they become internalized once repression operates. The other is internalized through repressed fantasies. It is repression that inaugurates sexuality and leads to the constitution of the unconscious fantasy. The excitation emanating from the adult's unconscious fantasies creates an intrusive element in a minor way. However, the excitation can be very traumatic when it concerns sexual aggression coming from the adult. In the fantasy of 'a child is being beaten', Laplanche (1999) draws our attention to the message of the father beating a young brother or sister, a message that is implanted in the ego and requires to be translated. The child faces the imperative of a continuous work of translation, that is the elaboration of the excitation. In the fundamental anthropological situation, the adult gives messages to the child without being aware that they are compromised by the *sexual*, that is by his/her infantile sexuality, which has the power of exciting, thus seducing the child. This is why Laplanche names the child's encounter with the adult as general seduction, in opposition to the restricted seduction referring to a sexual aggression committed by the adult. Infantile sexuality shapes adult sexuality by the indestructible character of the original objects and its polymorphically perverse pleasures.

In opposition to Laplanche's point of view with respect to the pre-scriptive nature of the assignment of gender, Paul Denis (2015) conceives a certain plasticity of the identifications in the building of gender. He parts from Stoller's views on the early organization of a 'core gender identity' (Stoller, 1964). The experience of oneself as masculine or feminine is built on what Stoller names as the 'gender identity nucleus', which consists of the conviction that one's sexual assignment is anatomically and eventually psychologically correct. This would be the first step towards the constitution of the individual's gender identity. Denis remarks that at the beginning the child's sexuality is form-less and there is no sexual differentiation between the mother and the father. The difference between them is made of qualities: their smell, the way they hold the child and other nuances. The young child of both sexes identifies with the mother on the basis of sameness, an aspect that indicates her early influence in terms of the maternal and the feminine. Denis remarks that the building of gender constitutes the first level of organization and precedes the recognition of the anatomical sex that he names a 'Copernican revolution'. The recognition of the anatomical difference of the other leads to the recognition of the child's own sex: male *or* female. Hence, anatomical sex would be objective, whereas gender is subjective because of the polymorphism of identifications with both parents. A person can be feminine in some aspects and masculine in others, as a result of his or her psychic bisexuality. This proposition reminds us of the distinction made by Freud between object–choice and sexual attitude. In 'The psychogenesis of a case of homosexuality in a woman' (1920a), Freud indicates that object–choice and sexual attitude do not necessarily coincide.

> Experience, however, proves the contrary: a man with predominantly male characteristics and also masculine in his erotic life may still be inverted in respect to his object, loving only men instead of women. A man in whose character feminine attributes obviously predominate, who may, indeed, behave in love like a woman, might be expected, from this feminine attitude, to choose a man for his love–object; but he may nevertheless be heterosexual, and show no more inversion in respect to his object than an average normal man. The same is true of women, here also mental sexual character and object–choice do not necessarily coincide.
>
> (1920a, p. 170)

Despite the immersion of the child in a gender pattern transmitted by the parents, their attitude may play complementary or contradictory roles. This is why Denis (2015) proposes a 'gender complex' made of two elements, one masculine and the other feminine. At this point, we can identify a major difference between Denis and Laplanche with respect to the constitution of gender identity. While for Denis gender identity is the result of the identification *with* both parents, for Laplanche it is the product of the identification of the child *by* the parent or the *socius* which precedes the identification *with* the parents.

The feminine as the primordial element

Laplanche's conception of gender as the result of the identification *by* the parent is well illustrated by Winnicott's (1971) male patient, who had been received as a girl at his birth. This case shows at the same time that the parent assigns to the child 'the sex of a fantasized anatomy', independently of the objective anatomy. In this male patient, a dissociation had been produced between the feminine elements and the masculine elements. The mother's madness that consisted in seeing a girl where there was a boy, had been enacted by the analyst. This time it was Winnicott who had seen a girl lying on the couch when he knew that there was a man in this place. The patient had talked about his penis-envy and the analyst had thought that only girls could express their penis-envy. The elaboration realized by the analyst in this session and in the following ones, enabled the patient to overcome the dissociation operating in his psychic reality and to accept his bisexuality, which would reflect a quality of a total self. After years of analysis, it was the first time that the patient could experience an authentic relation with the analyst and have the feeling of a sense of identity. Very curiously, it was this male patient who had allowed Winnicott to discover the importance of the feminine element, present at the beginning of life, from which emerges the masculine element. The feminine element, as the initial bond with the mother, would be the major force that allows the narcissistic foundation of the subject. Analytic work with transsexual patients suffering from a sense of basic identity shows us that the feminine element is primordial for the identity. In relation to the analytic work realized with a transsexual patient who had changed from male to female, Danielle Quinodoz resorts to Winnicott's notion of the feminine:

> Winnicott, however, considers that the intensity of the initial bond with the mother permits the construction of a sexually neutral sense of basic identity along the lines that masculinity is a process that has to be initiated out of femininity, which is itself more in the nature of a 'state': 'The male element does while the female element ... *is*' (1966, p. 178).
>
> (Quinodoz, 1998, p. 97)

Here, the female element corresponds to the primary identification with the mother and is valid for both sexes: 'the pure female element relates to the breast (or to the mother) in the sense of the *baby becoming the breast (or mother), in the sense that the object is the subject*' (Winnicott, 1971, p. 79, emphasis in original).

From primary femininity to genital femininity

If we interrogate what constitutes the core of femininity, we see that psychoanalysts have given different answers to this question. Many psychoanalysts coincide with the idea of an early feminine phase, product of the primary identification with the mother. Melanie Klein (1932) conceives an early feminine phase for both the girl and the boy, whereas Stoller (1964) speaks of a 'femininity canvas' that results from the fusion of the child with the mother and leads to the constitution of a core of gender identity. The boy would have to elaborate the feminine element in the building of his male identity. Emilce Dio Bleichmar (2006), who situates the girl's feminine identity in the early identification with the maternal, remarks that it is not an inborn femininity (Klein, 1932; Jones, 1935) nor is it due to the vaginal feelings and recognition of her genital organs (Elise, 1997). Florence Guignard (1999), on her part, defines 'the primary maternal' as the identification of the child with the maternal capacity for *reverie* and 'the primary feminine' as the identification of the child with the maternal desire for the father. Hence, from the beginning the father is included as the mother's object of desire, a process that lays the path for the girl's genital femininity once she recognizes sexual difference. In this sense, the girl identifies with the mother who is a woman and has a sexual life. The feminine for Catherine Chabert (2003, 2019) consists of the common infantile core for both sexes, created by the early representations of the maternal that will be determinant in the constitution of a sexuated subject. Hence, the feminine is synonymous with the infantile to the extent that it provokes images of passivity and helplessness. Both Chabert and André underline the child's passivity with respect to the mother's seduction. Laplanche (1985, 2011), Chabert (2003, 2019) and André (1995) concur in the fact that the mother's unconscious sexual fantasies leave traces in the child's erotogenic zones, due to the excitation they provoke. André notes that the erotogenic zones, through which the mother's unconscious sexual fantasies break in, become the point of conjunction of the seduced child and the feminine position. Here, lies the most archaic point of anchorage: the seduced child is the child penetrated through the orifices. The 'penetrated-being of the seduced child' anticipates the 'penetrated-being of femininity' (André, 1995, p. 111, my own translation). Thus, this early feminine position relative to the mother's seduction anticipates the girl's genital femininity, constituted after the establishment of sexual differentiation. The conception of Laplanche, Chabert and André with respect to the early feminine position of the child concerns the sexual drive, whereas for Winnicott the pure female element refers to primary identification in a narcissistic sense and does not include the parents', particularly the mother's sexuality. In this sense, it is impossible to conceive the girl's femininity solely on a narcissistic base in identification with the mother.

References

André, J. (1995). *Aux origines féminines de la sexualité*. Paris: PUF.

André, J. (2017). Quel genre de sexe? In: J. André (Ed.), *Quel genre de sexe?* Paris: PUF.

Butler, J. (1990). *Gender trouble*. New York: Routledge.

Butler, J. (1993). *Bodies that matter*. New York: Routledge.

Chabert, C. (2003). *Féminin mélancolique*. Paris: PUF.

Chabert, C. (2019). Féminin pluriel. Hystérie, masochisme ou mélancolie? *Revue française de psychanalyse*, *83*:3, 811–823.

Denis, P. (2015). Gender as heritage of the first qualitative differentiation. In: E. Abrevaya & F. Thomson-Salo (Eds.), *Homosexualities*. London: Karnak.

Dejours, C. (2003). Pour une théorie psychanalytique de la différence des sexes. Introduction à l'article de Jean Laplanche. In: A. Green, I. Grubrich-Simitis, J. Laplanche & J-G. Schimek (Eds.), *Sur la théorie de la séduction*. Paris: Editions In Press.

Dio Bleichmar, E. (2018). The place of motherhood in primary femininity. In: A.M. Alizade (Ed.), *Motherhood in the twenty-first century*. New York: Routledge.

Elise, D. (1997). Primary femininity, bisexuality and the female ego ideal. A re-examination of female developmental theory. *Psychoanalytic quarterly*, *66*, 489–517.

Ferenczi, S. (1932). *The confusion of tongues between adult and child: Final contributions to the problems and methods of psycho-analysis*. New York: Brunner-Mazel, 1980.

Foucault, M. (1980). *Herculine Barbin: Being the recently discovered memoirs of a nineteenth century hermaphrodite*. New York: Vintage.

Freud, S. (1905d). *Three essays on the theory of sexuality*. SE, 7: 125–243.

Freud, S. (1920a). The psychogenesis of a case of homosexuality in a woman. *SE*, *18*: 147–172.

Freud, S. (1931b). Female sexuality. *SE*, *21*: 225–243.

Freud, S. (1933a). Femininity. *New introductory lectures on psychoanalysis. SE*, *22*: 112–135.

Green, A. (1973). Le genre neutre. In: J.-B. Pontalis (Ed.), *Bisexualité et différence des sexes*. Paris: Gallimard.

Guignard, F. (1999). Maternel ou féminin? Le 'roc d'origine' comme gardien du tabou de l'inceste avec la mère. In: J. Schaeffer, M. Cournut-Janin, S. Faure-Pragier, F. Guignard (Eds.), *Clefs pour le féminin*. Paris: PUF.

Jones, E. (1935). Early female sexuality. *International journal of psychoanalysis*, *16*, 263–273.

Klein, M. (1932). *The psycho-analysis of children*. London: Hogarth.

Laplanche, J. (1980). *Castration. Symbolisations*. Paris: PUF.

Laplanche, J. (1985). *Life and death in psychoanalysis*. Baltimore, MD: Johns Hopkins University Press.

Laplanche, J. (1999). *Essays on otherness*. London: Routledge.

Laplanche, J. (2003). Le genre, le sexe, le sexual. In: A. Green, I. Grubrich-Simitis, J. Laplanche, J-G. Schimek (Eds.), *Sur la théorie de la séduction*. Paris: Editions In Press.

Laplanche, J. (2007). Le genre, le sexe, le sexual. *Sexual*, Paris: PUF.

Laplanche, J. (2011). *Freud and the sexual*. New York: International Psychoanalytic Books.

Laufer, L. (2010). La fabrique du corps sexué. *Recherches en psychanalyse*, *10*, 231–241.

Lévy, J.M. (2019). Ombres et lumières de la bisexualité. *Revue française de psychanalyse,* *83*:5, 1421–1476.

Quinodoz, D. (1998). A fe/male transsexual patient in psychoanalysis. *International journal of psychoanalysis, 79,* 95–111.

Roiphe, H. & Galenson, E. (1981). *Infantile origins of sexual identity.* New York: International Universities Press.

Stoller, R.J. (1964). A contribution to the study of gender identity. *International journal of psychoanalysis, 45*: 220–226.

Stoller, R.J. (1994). *Sex and gender. The development of masculinity and femininity.* London: Taylor & Francis.

Winnicott, D.W. (1971). The split-off male and female elements to be found in men and women. In: *Playing and reality.* London: Tavistock Publications.

6 The feminine and new conceptions of motherhood

The interrogation of gender

Social changes in contemporary societies as well as the evolution of mentalities oblige us to revise our psychoanalytic theories and interrogate a phallocentric conception of psychoanalysis, along with its underlying notions such as penis-envy, the phallus, castration and so on. Susann Heenen-Wolff (2017) warns us against the danger of adopting theories that are imbedded in normative points of view on heterosexuality, homosexuality, masculinity and femininity and invites us to be critical about them. We have attained a certain degree of cultural and social development that has brought about notable transformations in terms of female subjectivity, even in countries that are not part of the occidental world. The interrogation of gender has become central in most of the cultural productions and in terms of women's rights and social access, such as the possibility of becoming a football player in Saudi Arabia or acquiring a driver's licence in Iran. In this context, maternity is not the inevitable and unique solution for *jouissance* and an equation between maternity and femininity is reductive to the extent that nowadays quite a significant number of women choose not to be mothers. In case a correspondence can be established between maternity and femininity, it cannot be considered only for heterosexual women, as such a correspondence would leave out homosexual women who wish to become mothers. On the other hand, we know that for a significant number of women motherhood continues to represent a principal source of gratification.

The analysis of the feminine, notes Leticia Glocer Fiorini (2019), requires the recognition of its multiple significations, such as 'the feminine', 'the woman', 'the mother', 'female sexuality' and 'femininity'. Despite these categories not being equivalent, they are, however, connected to each other on the conceptual map. She proposes to take into consideration the process of subjectivation on the basis of a paradigm of hyper-complexity that includes plurality, multiplicity and heterogeneity. In the absence of such a paradigm, the feminine would be reduced to a unique signification. A paradigm of hyper-complexity should inevitably include the binary logic,

DOI: 10.4324/9781003232261-6

that is the dualism inherent in the masculine and the feminine, which is deeply anchored in our representations and traverses culture and language. But at the same time we should be able to go beyond the binary logic and examine the post-binary logics that can help us understand the actual tendencies with respect to sexuality and gender, as well as the multiplicity of the subject's positions with respect to desire. 'The tales of the city', a series on Netflix (2019), illustrates the idea of the multiplicity of the subject's positions with respect to desire, an aspect that can be seen through a transsexual's erotic life. Initially as a female, she had formed a couple with a lesbian. After having undergone a sex-change, she became anatomically a man but at that point he had the feeling that he had lost his female part in his new male identity. He wished to experience his sexuality with male partners but he still felt attached to his former female·partner and longed for her. The ironical question is raised by his mother, depicted as a Hispanic and traditional character. She is very happy to think that her child, who has changed into a man now, can procreate with his former female partner, hence providing her the opportunity to become a grandmother. We can clearly see that the change that has converted the transsexual into a man cannot efface what has been constructed till then in the subjective sphere and in that of desire. Bernard Penot (2001) notes that the expansion of the function of the subject in analysis, conceived essentially as the subject of desire, results from the conjunction of the drive energy and the dimension of significance. Leticia Glocer Fiorini envisages the construction of subjectivity in the intersection of (1) the biological body, which is never solely biological, (2) the plurality of identifications including those referring to gender and (3) the subject's desire. We would add to this triad the dimension of significance, without which it is impossible to consider the process of subjectivation.

Leticia Glocer Fiorini, who proposes a paradigm of hyper-complexity in her approach to the feminine, integrates sublimation as part of 'itineraries of desire'. Her proposition seems essential to us to the extent that we confer a pivotal role to sublimation in terms of desire. Leticia Glocer Fiorini (2019) gives an interesting example of a female patient. In Ms G, sublimation had become the major source of self-realization. Shortly after having given birth to her daughter, she had returned to her professional work, which highly engaged her. Her psychoanalyst found that the aspects relative to sublimation had a greater force than those related to her motherhood. At this point we can see the impact that the woman analyst's implicit theories, which can be oppressive, can have, provoking feelings of guilt in the woman patient. Can a woman who has become a mother freely express that her professional work has a great impact on her life and has even become her priority? Can the woman analyst understand such a patient despite her own conception of maternity and femininity differing from that of her patient? It is crucial for the woman analyst to be able to recognize the singularity of each woman patient and her desire. Sublimation constitutes one of the privileged means for self-expression, self-creation and growth in women, despite Freud not recognizing it as a real possibility for them. However, sublimation constitutes a red thread in this book as a source of *jouissance* for women. The production of cultural objects, which include art and science, corresponds to a principle means of self-realization in women, who can have their place in the public sphere and express themselves by means of their creations. Freud had related what he considered as a poor capacity for sublimation in women to the lack of castration anxiety, hence basing himself on the model of male sexuality. Despite his acknowledgement of the theoretical contributions of some women analysts in his time, and thus of their capacity for sublimation, he qualified them as being phallic and expressions of masculinity. Even if we suppose that there is a phallic aspect underlying these contributions, we consider that sublimation in women concerns essentially the erogenous female body and the affects. We will be discussing in the next chapter the question of sublimation in women, situating it in terms of female sexuality.

New conceptions of motherhood

The social revolution at the end of the twentieth century brought about the 'right to choose' for women, giving them the possibility to become mothers or not. The repudiation of motherhood, which used to be considered by the psychoanalyst as an expression of the masculinity complex, hence became a feministic posture. In this sense, motherhood is no longer a privileged expression of femininity. However, in spite of the disjunction of motherhood and femininity, the ardent desire to become a mother can come to the forefront of the new types of families, such as those composed of a single parent living with his/her children or those that are formed by parents of the same sex. An impressive change concerning the reproductive technology has occurred, offering the opportunity to have children to infertile women or men in couples, to single heterosexual and lesbian women as well as to homosexual couples. These changes have shaken the basis of our perception and knowledge in terms of gender, sexuality and motherhood. In spite of being well informed about the urge to be a mother or a father, we still lack a reflexion of the way a lesbian couple experiences its femininity. The introduction of the 'birth other' into the reproductive process involves a woman donating her eggs or offering her womb or a man donating his sperm, a process in which sexuality and procreation are dissociated. In this sense, multiple disjunctions take place, some of which are between maternity and femininity or between sexual desire and procreation. However, the absence of sexual desire leading to conception does not exclude the maternal or paternal desire for a child and the satisfaction that the child brings. On the other hand, the absence of the sexual union of the couple does not mean that the conception of a child is exempt from sexual fantasies. Among several examples that Diane Ehrensaft gives, we note that Alexis, a single woman, had fantasies with respect to the donor who was gay. During the period of insemination, she fantasized that she could make the child with the donor in the 'old-fashioned way' and had erotic fantasies about his body.

> Surrounded by a culture that promotes monogamy and coupled love and emerging from a childhood filled with primal scenes and triangulated Oedipal dramas, the deeply imbedded scenario of man, woman, sex and pregnancy remains stable, if not immutable. Fantasies of illicit sex, adultery, and a ménage à trois can take a mother by surprise.
>
> (Ehrensaft, 2006, p. 25)

Maureen could not reveal to her daughter that her father was not the biological father and that she had been conceived by a donor's sperm. She imagined that her daughter would think that she had been unfaithful to her husband and had sex with another man. In fact, it was Maureen's fantasy that she had had her daughter by another man. The presence of sexual fantasies concerning the 'birth other' reflects the extent to which conception is imbedded with the sexual even if it contradicts its concrete reality. Assisted reproductive technology implies, as Jodie Davies (1998) suggests, the desire of a person or a couple to have a child but also the help of one or more persons, through the use of another woman's eggs or womb or another man's sperm. As we have seen in this discussion, the absence of the sexual union leading to conception does not remove or efface the 'primacy of the sexual' (Laplanche, 2007) in psychic life nor its polymorphic aspects. The unconscious fantasies of the adult intervene to the extent that conception always implies the presence of the sexual, hence the fantasy of the primal scene.

Cooper and Glazer (1994) give the example of a woman who had felt very disconcerted when she fantasized a sexual scene between her husband and her female friend who had donated her eggs. 'They are making the embryo/baby while I wait, then I'll carry *their* embryo that I didn't contribute to making' (Cooper & Glazer, 1994, p. 233). This sexual scene had awakened the fantasy of the primal scene relative to her parents and her exclusion as a child from what went on in the parental bedroom. The turmoil created by the rivalry with the 'birth other', perceived as a sexual competitor, can lead to the denial of the donor. Parents can reach that degree of denial by means of reducing the donator to a partial object, such as the womb, the eggs or sperm, a denial that Diane Ehrensaft (2010, p. 1110) names 'immaculate illusion'. This defence does not necessarily protect the mother-to-be from the anxiety arising from her unconscious or conscious fantasies about the role of the other woman or the other man in the conception. But sometimes the opposite can be noted when the mother fantasizes the sperm-donor as a lover. Marlene, a single lesbian mother, had unintentionally found out the identity of the sperm-donor. She imagined herself as going to his office to show him the pictures of 'their' daughter. In the situation where there was no father for her daughter, she needed to compensate for this by filling this place with her fantasies. In this sense, nothing impeded the lesbian mother from fantasizing about a man, a father, as the object of her desire. In other words, the female subject's homosexual object–choice does not exclude her desire for a man, hence illustrating the different positions that can exist with respect to desire as part of psychic bisexuality.

We can see the degree to which assisted reproductive technologies introduce different imaginary scenarios with respect to sexuality and maternity. In cases where the mother has been infertile, the female donor continues to exist in her fantasies even if she has never met her. Diane Ehrensaft (2006, p. 30) defines as 'mother envy' the feelings of the mother-to-be with respect to the female donor, who is imagined as a fertile woman who can offer her eggs without any restrictions. Frequently the mother-to-be has no time to mourn her infertility as she is caught by a sense of urgency in order to realize her motherhood. Sylvie Faure-Pragier (2011) concurs with Ehrensaft, as she considers that the urge to have a child by means of assisted reproductive technology does not leave time for mourning. However, multiple attempts to get pregnant can impede the acceptance that the age for conception has already been reached. This was the case of Nadèje, who had adopted a child after having attempted for ten years to get pregnant and had ended by not being able to establish a deep tie with her adopted child. The latter had represented a substitute that could not satisfy her because through all these years she had not renounced the fantasy of having her own child. Faure-Pragier (2011) also discusses examples of fathers for whom their infertility is devastating and they need to keep secret the fact that a sperm-donor has intervened. We can speak here of 'father envy', as the corollary to 'mother envy' (Ehrensaft, 2006), in which the sperm-donor is fantasized as a very potent man. In situations in which a donor has intervened for both sexes, fathers can be more fragile when compared with mothers. In cases in which the egg-donor has become necessary due to the woman's sterility caused by a genetic anomaly, the painful feeling that the woman experiences because of her sterility can be compensated by her pregnancy. The latter offers the opportunity to experience herself as fertile and the objective reality of sterility can be forgotten, whereas in the case of an infertile man there is no such possible compensation.

Chantal, a homosexual woman who lived as a couple with her female partner, had considered having a child with a man with whom she had a satisfying sexual relation. However, conception had not been possible with him. Faure-Pragier (2011) remarks that her strong attachment to the mother, who had never overcome her own mourning, had not permitted Chantal to differentiate herself from the mother. Faure-Pragier (2011) remarks that primary homosexuality in its passive aspects had been repressed, leading to the enactment of a homosexual object–choice. The latter seemed to assure a defence against her awareness of her passionate attachment to the mother, which impeded a feminine identification with her. The lack of a feminine identification meant that Chantal could not identify with a mother who desired the father, resulting in the impossibility of conceiving a child with her male friend. We think that the father's role in the femininity of his daughter is as important as the mother's to the extent that he can recognize and appreciate his daughter's feminine aspects. However, he can be assured of this role with respect to his daughter with the condition that he is the object of the mother's desire. It is only then that the daughter can identify with the mother who desires the father. Chantal's longing for a child came as an attempt at reparation of a femininity that could not be realized. The representation of the child assured the return to the primitive, fusional, idealized mother. Finally, Chantal was able to mourn her infertility and adopt a girl that she was able to love. Faure-Pragier (2011) regretted that the adoption could not be realized by Chantal and her companion, due to French legislation that requires the woman to be single. Despite a child not being able to have two mothers, Faure-Pragier (2011) considers that she can have a mother and a godmother, that is another parent who has the same rights over the child and in case of separation of the couple, the child would not be raised by one parent only.

Ken Corbett (2003) examines several problems from the perspective of the child who comes from families composed of homosexual couples or multiparental or monoparental families. How can the analyst manage and explain to the child when his or her conception has been different from that of traditional families, particularly when it concerns homosexual couples? How to explain to the child that two women can reproduce but each of them would need a man or a sperm-donor for a conception to take place? In case of a single parent, the challenge would be the creation of a triangulated space composed of the parent, the child and the donor as a total object and not only as a giver of sperms. The analyst confronts the necessity to deal with the parents' guilt feelings and anxiety as well as the child's disorientation, specially when beginning school. The child and the parents would have to face the dominant normative logic in their environment. Corbett (2003) proposes to the parents and the child the construction of a 'family novel' that confers the feeling of belonging to that particular family. How can a family build its own story? The example of Andy, aged seven and living with the biological mother and the social mother, serves to illustrate the way the analyst tries to think about and elaborate these problems with the child. Andy's process is highly illustrative of the conflicts undergone by a child coming from a family composed of two women. But this case also obliges us to rethink the categories of the masculine and the feminine with respect to the homosexual couple.

Andy felt ashamed because of the masculine appearance of R.J., who was his social mother. He was not her biological child and he found himself in situations where he had to explain that R.J. was his mother without being his biological mother. However, Andy liked R.J.'s active physical presence with which he identified, as she could share Andy's interests as a boy, like sports or games. These contradictory feelings made him suffer and provoked anger with respect to her. On the other hand, she played an important parental role by training her son's football team and participating in the parents association in school. At the same time she could be sensitive to Andy's psychological needs. The analyst had to work with R.J., communicating to her Andy's desire to have a mother who resembled a girl but also knew how to play like a boy. R.J. knew that she could not realize Andy's desire but she stayed open to his desire as well as to his anger and hate that resulted from the impossibility of realizing his own desire. His biological mother, Ellen, also provoked his anger when she explained to the others that she was lesbian. Andy wished his mother would pretend to be 'normal' and not declare her homosexuality so openly. When Ellen and R.J were confronted with situations of verbal aggression with respect to their homosexuality, they tried to fight against it by discussing with Andy what it meant to be 'different' and to be a minority. They emphasized the importance of being tolerant to others who are not similar to them. In this sense, the discrimination they experienced did not provoke their isolation as a family. On the contrary, they tried to be open to persons or communities that were discriminated against and reflected on these problems with Andy, hence giving him the opportunity to go beyond the rejection and transform these painful situations.

At one point of the therapeutic process, the analyst had to work with Andy's desire to know about his biological father and fathers in general. He needed to assure himself that his curiosity about his father would not cause pain to his mothers. Hence, the analyst worked with Andy and his mothers regarding the collective fantasies with respect to the donor. The analytic work revealed that the couple had repressed the lively fantasies shared with respect to him before Andy's birth. As they had some information on the donor, they fantasized that he had similar characteristics to significant members of each other's family. R.J. imagined that he was like Ellen's younger sister, who had achieved graduate studies in mathematics, and Ellen imagined that he played violoncello like R.J.'s brother. The interesting thing here is that these significant relatives, objects of desire and admiration, did not belong to their own family but to that of the partner. Based on the information they had on him, they expressed that they had almost 'fallen in love' with him and had given him the name Tim. Their homosexuality did not impede their fantasizing about a man that they imagined as being attractive. These fantasies indicate the extent to which psychic life has an incredible plasticity. They did not deny the donor, in contrast to others who can reduce the donor to sperm, that is to a partial object. After Andy's birth, his parents had felt the necessity to silence their fantasies because they thought that to speak openly of them could be stimulating their son's curiosity as well as his desire to meet the father. Analytic work made it possible for the parents to consider that, despite not being able to realize Andy's wish to meet the father, they could offer the possibility of dreaming about him and talking about him, as they imagined him. In other words, they could have their familial reveries with respect to him.

When working with homosexual couples or a single parent that has had a child by means of a donor's sperm or eggs, Faure-Pragier (2011) remarks that the emphasis should not be on the reality of the conception but on the possibility of fantasizing around it. The psyche has an extraordinary capacity for weaving the facts into a story even in the case where the real does not provide for it. Nothing impeded Andy from fantasizing about his father; however, this was only possible on the condition that his parents participated in building their family story together. In families composed of homosexual parents, sexual difference can continue to exist even if the parents do not represent it and the difference between generations exists anyway. In the case where the child has no possibility of building a primal scene between the father and the mother, Faure-Pragier (2011)proposes a *new kind of primal fantasy* referring to the parents' ardent desire to have a child, a fantasy that would have a structuring effect on the child's psyche. Andy expressed his wish but also his anxiety with respect to growing up and becoming a man. The fact that he had a male analyst facilitated the transference of his desires and fantasies with respect to the father. On the other hand, he had to elaborate the fact that in his family it was R.J. who played the role of the father. A certain degree of complexity arose in this situation as R.J. was also his mother. Despite Andy's suffering with respect to the impossibility of meeting his father at least till the age of eighteen, he also knew that his parents were open-minded and could face the difficulties brought about by the kind of family they had. A question arises in this discussion as to the significance of having two mothers. In this case, different aspects relative to motherhood can be represented by each of them and would not be concentrated only on one mother. There was a time when children were raised in extensive families with other close members, such as their grandparents, aunts, uncles and cousins. However, the development of the family into a nuclear family eliminated the auxiliaries and placed the child's psychological needs at the centre of the parents' attention. The kibbutz experience in Israel or similar collective experiences that took place in the Soviet Union after the revolution of 1917 exemplified the value accorded to socialization and to an education realized by multiple mothers. In non-traditional families in which the child faces difficulties in the absence of the father, as in Andy's case, or in the absence of the mother as would be the case with a couple of male homosexuals, it is important to consider a central point about which Faure-Pragier (2011) reminds us: the extraordinary capacity for auto-organization as well as the psychic plasticity of the human being. It is possible to conceive the child's or the adult's psychological needs in a creative way, in a context that requires invention and a fresh look without operating dichotomies.

References

Cooper, S. & Glazer, E. (1994). *Beyond infertility: The new paths to parenthood*. New York: Lexington Books.

Corbett, K. (2003). Le roman familial non traditionnel. *Revue française de psychanalyse, 67*: 1, 197–218.

Davies, J. M. (1998). Thoughts on the nature of desires: The ambiguous, the transitional, and the poetic. *Psychoanalytic dialogues, 8*, 805–823.

Ehrensaft, D. (2006) Motherhood in a fertile new world. In: A.M. Alizade (Ed.), *Motherhood in the twenty-first century*. New York: Routledge.

Ehrensaft, D. (2010). Quand parfois pour faire un bébé, il faut être trois ou quatre, voire plus. *Revue française de psychanalyse, 74*:4, 1101–1123.

Faure-Pragier, S. (2011). Rester psychanalyste face au chaos des nouvelles filiations. *Revue française de psychanalyse, 75*:4, 1063–1080.

Glocer Fiorini, L. (2019). Vers une déconstruction du 'féminin': discours, logiques et pouvoir. Les implications théorico-cliniques. *Revue française de psychanalyse, 83*:3, 825–839.

Heenen-Wolff, S. (2017). *Contre la normativité en psychanalyse*. Paris: Editions In Press.

Laplanche, J. (2007). *Sexual*. Paris: PUF.

Penot, B. (2001). *La passion du sujet freudien. Entre pulsionnalité et signifiance*. Paris: Erès.

7 Femininity, desire and sublimation

The nature of the sexual drive and sublimation

Following *Three essays* (1905d), Freud underlined the problematic nature of human sexuality. In 'On the universal tendency to debasement in the sphere of love', he remarks that something in the nature of the sexual drive impedes the realization of complete satisfaction and enumerates the obstacles to it.

> Firstly, as a result of the diphasic onset of object–choice, and the inter-position of the barrier against incest, the final object of the sexual instinct is never any longer the original object but only a surrogate for it. Psycho-analysis has shown us that when the original object of a wishful impulse has been lost as a result of repression, it is frequently represented by an endless series of substitutive objects none of which, however, brings full satisfaction.
>
> (1912d, pp. 188–189)

The sexual drive cannot attain full satisfaction due not only to the exigent demands of civilization but also to its particular nature. However, thanks to sublimation this absolute impossibility becomes the source of the most crea-tive, artistic and intellectual productions. In *Three essays*, Freud finds out that the polymorphic perverse disposition of infantile sexuality can be considered as 'the source of a number of our virtues' (1905d, p. 239), an idea that he also discusses in 'On the universal tendency to debasement in the sphere of love'

> The very incapacity of the sexual instinct to yield complete satisfac-tion as soon as it submits to the first demands of civilization becomes the source, however, of the noblest cultural achievements which are brought into being by ever more extensive sublimations of its instinc-tual components.
>
> (Freud, 1912d, p. 190)

Freud re-examines the issue of sexual satisfaction in *Civilization and its dis-contents*: 'Sometimes one seems to perceive that it is not only the pressure

DOI: 10.4324/9781003232261-7

of civilization but something in the nature of the function itself which denies us full satisfaction and urges us along other paths' (1930a, p. 105). If the impossibility to access complete sexual satisfaction becomes the source of sublimation, however, this had historically been the prerogative of men. So, the study of sublimation in women becomes an attempt to invert this conception that consisted in confining women to a unique role, that of motherhood. In this sense, it is necessary to discuss sublimation in the context of female sexuality and from the viewpoint of the specificity of the Oedipus complex in the girl.

The question of supplementary *jouissance*

Patrick Guyomard (2018) defines Lacan's contribution to psychoanalysis as a return to Freud, a return to the signification of his work. Lacan's (1966) theoretical conception represents a continuity of Freud's work but also a rupture, as illustrated by his point of view with respect to female sexuality. Lacan is Freudian with his emphasis on the phallus but in rupture with Freud when he notes the impossibility of situating female sexuality in the perspective of 'the universal of the oedipal schema' (Guyomard, 2018, p. 909). In his seminar *Les formations de l'inconscient* (1957–1958), Lacan discusses the notion of the mascarade, which points to the division between the phallic functions and the feminine functions and re-examines it in his seminar *Les quatre concepts fondamentaux de la psychanalyse* (1964). He notes that beyond the notions of activity and passivity used to designate respectively the masculine and the feminine, the mascarade would better define the sexual attitude of a woman. In *Les formations de l'inconscient*, he examines the Freudian definition of the phallic phase. Both the girl and the boy desire the mother and the desire at this point can only be possible if the girl, like the boy, has the fantasy of possessing a phallus. In other words, the little girl presents herself in a masculine position with respect to the mother. However, when compared with the boy, something much more complex has to take place in her, something that can assure her passage to the feminine position. We know that Freud does not envisage a feminine position for the girl before the onset of puberty, as he conceives her in a symmetrical way to the boy. Lacan does not share Freud's idea with respect to the absence of a feminine position in the girl and concurs with Jones' findings in 'Early female sexuality' (1935). Jones remarks that the phallic phase, which takes place after the resolution of the oedipal complex, assures a defensive function protecting the girl against the anxiety produced by her vaginal sensations. The little girl has a primitive perception of her vagina, which is the source of erotogenic sensations. The latter are repressed due to the anxiety of penetration aroused by the father. On the other hand, the vagina is the source of anxiety to the extent that it is not visible for her. In this sense, the clitoris serves as an external organ onto which she projects her anxiety that can reassure her, thanks to its visibility and the possibility of manipulating it. The phallic phase is temporary and disappears at the entry of puberty.

From then on, the girl needs external objects in reference to her body, with which she dresses her body. Objects, such as clothes and accessories, serve to reassure her and placate her anxiety, as they concern a displacement from the internal sexual organ to the external part of the body. The function assured by the mascarade would find its place on this level. Lacan (1957–1958) argues that the phallus intervenes as something necessary that can be exteriorized and represented and this is realized by the way the female body is dressed and exhibited. Monique Cournut-Janin (1998) agrees with Ernest Jones when she observes that the non-visibility of the girl's sex in the mirror and its hidden aspect generate anxiety, leading to the need to master it. The little girl would feel more exposed to a man's gaze, which tends to provoke the anxiety of penetration in her. She notes that hysteria becomes a way of organizing the affects, sensations and excitations related to the female body. Yet, there would be a risk of dilution in the image that the girl has of herself in the mirror to the extent that nothing psychically comes to organize it with respect to a principal organ, as would be the case of the boy with respect to his penis. The excitation projected onto the surface of the female body does not lead to an experience of unity. Or, the hysterical theatre or the mascarade would assure the externalization and representation of what is internal. Cournut-Janin makes a distinction between the feminine and femininity. While femininity is presented as something to be seen and *erected* as an unconscious defence against the anxiety arising from inside, the feminine is constituted more secretly under the cover of femininity. The idea of the feminine being secretly constituted evokes Winnicott's (1971) notion of the feminine. The authentic self, which leans on the primordial feminine, is silent. Some psychoanalysts have criticized the notion of the feminine in Winnicott indicating that it is exempt from sexuality. In this sense, the feminine in Winnicott would be constituted in an early identification with the mother and its value would be mainly narcissistic, whereas for Laplanche (1970), André (1995), Cournut-Janin (1998), Guignard (1999), Chabert (2003), Godfrind (2001) and Schaeffer (2000) the girl identifies with the mother, who is at the same time a woman and has an erotic life with the lover.

Cournut-Janin (1998) remarks that the division between the feminine and femininity confers a duality to female identity. While femininity concerns the surface of the body as something to be exhibited, the feminine involves the interior of the body along with the oral, anal and genital zones and the erotogenic sensations related to them. '*Femininity would be a way of playing with the phallic by borrowing its logic*' (Cournut-Janin, 1998, p. 89, my own translation, emphasis in original). In this sense, there is a phallic reference inherent in the bodily theatre that is displayed. The psychical organization of the feminine and its projection onto the surface of the body also becomes a way for a woman to protect herself against the melancholic. The feminine in both sexes, but particularly in women, would be related to a melancholic aspect inherent in separation from the primordial object, as noted by Kristeva (1992), Cournut-Janin (1999), Chabert (2003, 2019), Godfrind (2001, 2018). In 'Melancholy gender – Refused identification', Judith Butler situates the 'melancholic condition of the bodily ego in terms of the "loss" of the same-sexed object' (Butler, 1995, p. 165), loss which would be the consequence of the disavowal of a homosexual attachment in both sexes. She attributes the cause of a melancholic identification to the 'prevalent conditions of compulsory heterosexuality', placing at the same level the girl's separation from the mother and the boy's separation from the father. However, the mother is the first object, the primordial object of both the girl and the boy and the melancholic identification, in this case, would owe its nature to the separation from the primordial object.

Lacan remarks that during the sexual act, the *jouissance* of both the woman and the man is necessarily phallic and does not include the Other in terms of signification. It is only when the lovers are in love that the 'being of the other' comes to the forefront of the relation. Hence, love comes to fill the gap created by the lack of signification inherent in the sexual relation. In his seminar *Le transfert* (1960–1961), Lacan elaborates what is specific to falling in love and defines it as the desire of the Other. The latter, as the code of the symbolic, is distinguished from the 'other', the imaginary partner. In this sense, love essentially consists in experiencing it from the alterity of the partner. Alain Badiou concurs with Lacan, remarking that love leads to a fundamental experience of what constitutes the difference with the Other and to 'the idea that we can experiment the world from the point of view of difference' (Badiou & Truong, 2009, p. 26). However, a woman's satisfaction cannot be reduced to phallic satisfaction and there is something more that is related to signification. In his seminar *Encore* (1972–1973), Lacan examines the question that Freud had left out in terms of female sexuality: What does a woman want? He recourses to the idea of a *supplementary jouissance* beyond the phallus, an idea that will guide our discussion on female sexuality and lead us to the study in that case of two principle satisfactions in women, the maternal passion and sublimation. The term of *jouissance* was introduced by Lacan, who envisaged it in the articulation of desire with language, that is with signification. '*Jouissance* concerns desire, precisely the unconscious desire; this shows to what degree this notion goes beyond all consideration of affects, emotions and feelings and raises the question of a relation to the object that passes through the unconscious signifiers' (Chemama & Vandermersch, 2003, my own translation). However, *jouissance* is opposed to the satisfaction obtained by the discharge of the drive. The subject's desire is caught in the symbolic system and what is radically pursued in terms of satisfaction concerns *signification*. Lacan refers to mystics who, like women, exemplify a *jouissance* beyond the phallus that they experience in their body. Although Lacan refers to mystics who are women, he also has in mind mystics who are men. It is not via the intellect but through their bodies that they experience the *jouissance,* realized in the pursuit of knowledge and truth with respect to God and the universe.

The maternal passion

The *passion* of a woman for motherhood is a source of *jouissance* beyond the phallus and constitutes a sublimation but with the condition that the child does not become the object that comes to compensate her narcissistic needs and injuries. The title of Kristeva's book reflects a woman's solitude with respect to the phallic universe: *Seule, une femme* (2007). She remarks that the overemphasis of pregnancy by the cultural order serves to obliterate the passionate aspect of motherhood, which corresponds to the prototype of the bond of love.

> Maternity is a passion in the sense of *emotions (of attachment and aggressivity* to the foetus, to the baby, to the child) that are transformed into *love* (idealization, project of life over time, devotion, and so on), with its corollary of *hate* more or less attenuated.
> (Kristeva, 2007, p. 172, my own translation, emphasis in original)

The maternal passion as *the prototype of the love relation* would, at the same time, include the renunciation of passion and that is its paradox. In other words, the mother's necessity to expel and detach the child from herself is inherent in maternal passion. Green shares Kristeva's point of view with respect to maternal passion which he names 'maternal madness' and concurs with Winnicott, who defends the view that primary maternal preoccupation is a transitory state of madness. In *On private madness* Green (1996) examines this question in a chapter on passions and their vicissitudes, which is evocative of Freud's (1915c) paper 'Instincts and their vicissitudes'. The mother wishes to be the *'unique and incomparable'* object for the child, for whom everything is sacrificed in the most natural way. Maternal madness would constitute the prototype of all amorous relations. Green (1996) supposes the presence from the beginning of such a passion in the mother but also regards it as a vicissitude of the 'primordial Eros' in perversions, neurosis or the most developed forms of sublimation. Hence, passion undergoes distinct vicissitudes depending on whether it concerns perversions, neurosis or sublimations. Freud expresses a similar idea to that of Green. In *Leonardo da Vinci and a memory of his childhood,*he remarks that sublimation would constitute 'the rarest and the most perfect' vicissitude of Eros (1910c, p. 80).

Sublimation as a source of *jouissance*

It is significant that we make our entry into the question of sublimation via maternal passion. In her dedication to her child, the mother realizes the 'greatest *intensity of the drive'* (Kristeva, 2007). Both motherhood and sublimation share a common aspect to the extent that they provide a *jouissance* beyond the phallus and can be thought of in terms of passion. Motherhood is a sublimation at the service of civilization, an aspect that Freud affirms. Héritier (2001), on her part, argues that motherhood has great consequences for both humanity and civilization, remarking that women have the capacity to reproduce not only the identical but also the different. The 'scandal' here is that women have the capacity not only to reproduce daughters but also to procreate sons, who are sexually different from them and this is an aspect obliterated by society. However, as we speak of motherhood, we are well aware of the risks of its idealization and the perils of an ideology that confines women to the private sphere.

In *A room of one's own*, Virginia Woolf contemplates the necessary social and economic conditions that can assure a woman to be able to write fiction or create works of art. Among these minimal conditions, she enumerates earning money and having a room for herself. Until the nineteenth century, it was impossible for women in England to earn money, as the law denied them the right to possess what they had earned. Woolf takes into consideration the effect that poverty has on the mind and thinks of 'the safety and prosperity of the one sex and of the poverty and insecurity of the other and of the effect of tradition and of the lack of tradition upon the mind of a writer' (Woolf, 2001, p. 19). Men wrote in abundance on women, whereas women had no opportunity to write, and if they did, it was not about men:

> A very queer, composite being thus emerges. Imaginatively she is of the highest importance; practically she is completely insignificant. She pervades poetry from cover to cover; she is all but absent from history. She dominates the lives of kings and conquerors in fiction; in fact she was the slave of any boy whose parents forced a ring upon her finger; […] in real life she could hardly read, could scarcely spell, and was the property of her husband.
>
> (Woolf, 2001, p. 36)

In this sense, the ability to think and create is essential for women's freedom. Women thinkers have been able to conquer a field that has been historically defined as the prerogative of men and access to a different kind of satisfaction for themselves. Thus, it is possible to affirm that there are different ways to access femininity, an aspect that Lacan also specified in his discussion of Riviere's paper 'Womanliness as a mascarade' (1929). In contrast to Freud who defined motherhood as the destiny of women, Lou Andreas-Salomé and Simone de Beauvoir, among many other prominent women, brought different answers to the question of what a woman wants, showing that their philosophical, literary and intellectual work were indispensable for their identity as well as for their *jouissance*.

Femininity and intellectual production

A woman who stands out on the scene of history as a thinker is Lou Andreas-Salomé, who embodies both feminine qualities and the capacity for reflexion. In an interview given to France Culture, in the context of a radio programme presented on August 8, 2018 entitled 'Eroticism and feminism', the French historian and philosopher Geneviève Fraisse defines her as an interlocutor and a producer of thought. Andreas-Salomé was the interlocutor of prominent intellectuals such as Nietzsche, Rilke and Freud. At the beginning of the twentieth century, at a time when women scarcely wrote, Andreas-Salomé had already won a place in the intellectual circles as an essayist, critic, journalist, novelist and as one of the first women to write in academic journals. Her encounter with Freud and psychoanalysis took place in 1911, a year after the publication of her book *The Erotic* (2013). She was fifty years old and Freud was fifty-five. She was not a young woman but Freud was captured by this beautiful and passionate woman. We clearly see here that it is not the youth of a woman that arouses the desire of the other and that there is something more, something enigmatic in a woman's femininity that provokes desire. After having corresponded with Martha during their engagement, Lou Andreas-Salomé was the second woman with whom Freud maintained his correspondence, which he did over twenty-four years, between 1912 and 1936 (Freud & Andreas-Salomé, 1985). This epistolary exchange was as valuable as those he realized with Karl Abraham, Pfister, Arnold Zweig and Sandor Ferenczi. In the preface that Marie Moscovici wrote to Andreas-Salomé's (1980) book *L'amour du narcissisme*, she remarks that Lacan regarded Lou Andreas-Salomé's correspondence with Freud as a continuation of 'the fundamental conversation with Fliess' (Moscovici, 1980, pp. 31–32). Freud's interlocution with Lou Andreas-Salomé played a similar role to that realized with Fliess, but with the difference that it concerned the thought of an independent and free woman 'in love with love', as Freud expressed.

Freud's prejudices with regard to women had not impeded him from admiring Lou's capability of comprehension, intelligence and intuition. He consulted her on psychoanalytic issues and she occupied the place of the third party in the conflicts with Stekel, Adler, Jung and Rank. She had not been a mother and in this sense she represented the stranger for Freud, but still her views were very valuable to him. He sought Lou's consolation when he had not yet received the news of his son who was on the front, and also consulted her in matters concerning his family, specially with respect to Anna. He invited Lou to stay in their house so that she could spend some time with his daughter. It was after Lou's stay in their house that Anna had begun her analysis, in fact her impossible analysis with the father. Thus, Lou represented for Anna a model both as a thinker and as a woman analyst. She encouraged Anna to participate in theoretical discussions, which used to intimidate her. In a letter written to Lou on May 9, 1931, Freud notes that he is struck by what seems to be 'exquisitely feminine' in her intellectual work. Lou had sent him a copy of her book that she had written about him, on the occasion of his seventy-fifth anniversary. His letter came as an answer to Lou's letter of May 4, 1931, in which she expressed how intolerable her suffering was, knowing that he was still experiencing great pain after his operation for maxilla. This gives us an idea about Lou's maternal attitude and tenderness with respect to Freud. It was not only Freud's admiration of Lou but also her adoration of him that shaped their relationship. Lou died in 1937, at the age of eighty-six years, approximately two and a half years before Freud's death. In the obituary that Freud published after her death, he expressed how honoured they felt with Lou's contribution to psychoanalysis, realized in the last twenty-five years of her life, and that 'the decisive piece of her destiny as a woman' had been played in Vienna. In this sense, Freud could recognize that Lou's extraordinary qualities as an intellectual and psychoanalyst could be part of a woman's destiny. When he underlined the 'exquisitely feminine' aspect in her intellectual work, the conjunction of the two qualities, femininity and intellectual production, is significant not only in Freud's discourse but from our perspective too. The femininity inherent in Lou's intellectual work makes us think that she could situate herself in a desiring position with respect to love as well as to intellectual work and psychoanalysis. This would be the *supplementary jouissance* that Lacan speaks of in a woman.

The burning desire to write

Another woman who, as a thinker and writer, marks the scene of history, is Simone de Beauvoir. While Lou reclaimed the assumption of the difference and singularity with respect to men, de Beauvoir defended the equality of both sexes. Both of them had become feminists in spite of having lived in different historical periods and geographies. Andreas-Salomé was born in 1861 in St Petersburg and died in 1937 in Gottingen, whereas de Beauvoir was born in 1908 in Paris and died in 1986. In a similar way to Andreas-Salomé, who occupied a unique place in Freud's life, Simone de Beauvoir played a key role in Jean-Paul Sartre's intellectual life. She was 'a privileged reader' of his books, whose approval meant that he did not need to take into account the critics' opinion with respect to what he wrote. She was educated in a suffocating Catholic milieu and was twenty-one years old when she met Sartre, who was two years older than her. They were both studying for the aggregation in philosophy, which was exclusively masculine. Sartre had been accepted in the first position and de Beauvoir in the second and she was the youngest person to have ever taken the exam. She had confidence in herself and believed that by means of her talent and knowledge, she could open a place for herself among men. She had decided very early on to dedicate her life to intellectual activities and she wished to communicate and write about the situations that impressed her. She dreamt of writing a 'novel of her interior life'. She was passionate and stubborn and had the urge to overcome the obstacles that stood on her way and realize herself by accomplishing a work. In this sense, she felt that she had 'the heart of a woman and the brain of a man' (de Beauvoir, 1958, p. 413). Her search for happiness and freedom was inseparable from her pursuit of love and friendship. She envisaged love as a total engagement with a man, as would be her relation with Sartre.

Till her encounter with Sartre, she thought that she was radically different from others to the extent that she could not imagine a life without being able to write. She found out that Sartre was guided by the same motives as she was: writing was the reason for their lives as well as their passion and they shared the urge to write about their ideas. In de Beauvoir's case, this urge consisted in writing not only on philosophy and literature but also in a more intimate way on her childhood and the formative years of her youth and adulthood. Her burning desire to write had more weight than the love she could have for a man, as her love affair with Nelson Algren illustrates. At the age of 39, she had fallen in love with Nelson Algren whom she met on one of her trips to United States. He was also a writer and had proposed marriage to her, which she rejected in order not to be far away from Sartre. Having chosen Sartre meant that the work of reflexion and writing were vital for her as well as the bond of love that united them. These are aspects that point to questions with respect to female subjectivity that have not been sufficiently explored. For de Beauvoir, Sartre embodied both the love for a man and the passion for writing. In this sense, female identity cannot be reduced to a woman's love life with her companion nor to motherhood.

Simone de Beauvoir tries to define what had been her privilege as a writer, specially while writing *The second sex* (2014), and affirms that she had been able to combine her female condition with the capability of reasoning. The dedication of a woman to thinking and writing is historically a transgression because she is not in her traditional place, that of being a mother and a spouse, whose role is also to support the husband's achievements and realizations. What is the force that pushes a woman to undertake the act of thinking and writing and what is it that renders it so urgent? Among different forms of sublimation, writing realized by women is most enigmatic. In *A writer's diary*, Virginia Woolf notes:

> And yet oddly enough I scarcely want children of my own now. This insatiable desire to write something before I die, this ravaging sense of shortness and feverishness of life, make me cling, like a man on a rock, to my one anchor.
>
> (1981, p. 117)

'This insatiable desire to write...' characterizes both de Beauvoir's and Woolf's passions. Geneviève Fraisse opens her book *Le privilège de Simone de Beauvoir* with these lines:

> There is no hesitation, we are right away settled in history, the long history of women who think and the short history of women in the collective conquest of knowledge as well as that of all the singular *jouissances* attached to it.
>
> (Fraisse, 2018, p. 11, my own translation)

De Beauvoir's principal privilege consisted in knowing that she belonged to history, to philosophical and political history, as Fraisse interrogates the philosophical determination and the force underlying *The second sex*. 'To have the same reason as men and to want to benefit from it indicates a capacity, a right, but also and above all, a possible *jouissance*' (Fraisse, 2018, p. 24, my own translation). The issue of the equality of the sexes in the modern era, she notes, has encountered a principal obstacle: doubt with respect to women's reason. De Beauvoir not only appropriates the exercise of reason, showing that women can do so like men, but uses it as something to be enjoyed. In this sense, it is meaningful that a woman can dedicate herself to the pursuit of knowledge and to thinking and reasoning.

References

André, J. (1995). *Aux origines féminines de la sexualité*. Paris: PUF.

Andreas-Salomé, L. (1980). *L'amour du narcissisme*. Paris: Gallimard.

Andreas-Salomé, L. (2013). *The erotic*. London: Routledge.

Badiou, A. & Truong, N. (2009). *Eloge de l'amour*. Paris: Flammarion.

Butler, J. (1995). Melancholy gender: Refused identification. *Psychoanalytic dialogues, 5*, 165–180.

Chabert, C. (2003). *Féminin mélancolique*. Paris: PUF.

Chabert, C. (2019). Féminin pluriel: hystérie, masochisme ou mélancolie? *Revue française de psychanalyse, 83:3*, 811–823.

Chemama, R. & Vandermersch, B. (2003). *Dictionnaire de la psychanalyse*. Paris: Larousse.

Cournut-Janin, M. (1998). *Féminin et féminité*. Paris: PUF.

Cournut-Janin, M. (1999). Le noyau féminin mélancolique, tel qu'il se découvre dans l'analyse, et le plus souvent au décours d'une cure, voire d'une tranche. In: J. Schaeffer, M. Cournut-Janin, S. Faure-Pragier & F. Guignard (Eds.). *Clés pour le féminin*. Paris: PUF.

De Beauvoir, S. (1958). *Mémoires d'une fille rangée*. Paris: Gallimard.

De Beauvoir, S. (2014). *The second sex*. London: Vintage.

Fraisse, G. (2018). *Le privilège de Simone de Beauvoir*. Paris: Gallimard.

Freud, S. (1905d). *Three essays on the theory of sexuality*. SE: 7, 125–245.

Freud, S. (1910c). *Leonardo da Vinci and a memory of his childhood*. SE: 11, 63–137.

Freud, S. (1912d). On the universal tendency to debasement in the sphere of love. *SE: 11*, 179–190.

Freud, S. (1915c). Instincts and their vicissitudes. *SE: 14*, 117–140.

Freud, S. (1930a*). Civilization and its discontents. SE: 21*, 64–145.

Freud, S. & Andreas-Salomé, L. (1985). *Letters (1912–1936).* New York: W.W. Norton.

Godfrind, J. (2001). *Comment la féminité vient aux femmes.* Paris: PUF.

Godfrind, J. (2018). From bisexuality to the feminine. In: R. Jozef Perelberg (Ed.), *Psychic bisexuality.* London: Routledge.

Green, A. (1996). *On private madness.* London: Routledge.

Guignard, F. (1999). Maternel ou féminin? Le 'roc d'origine' comme gardien du tabou de l'inceste avec la mère. In: J. Schaeffer, M. Cournut-Janin, S. Faure-Pragier & F. Guignard. *Clés pour le féminin* (Eds.). Paris: PUF.

Guyomard, P. (2018). La parole, le sujet, le langage. *Revue française de psychanalyse, 82:4*, 908–916.

Héritier, F. (2001). Inceste et substance. Oedipe, Allen, les autres et nous. In: J. André (Ed.), *Incestes.* Paris: PUF.

Jones, E. (1935). Early female sexuality. *International journal of psychoanalysis, 16*, 263–273.

Kristeva, J. (1992). *Black sun: Depression and melancholia.* New York: Columbia University Press.

Kristeva, J. (2007). *Seule, une femme.* Paris: l'Aube.

Lacan, J. (1957–1958). *Le séminaire. Livre V. Les formations de l'inconscient.* Paris: Seuil, 1998.

Lacan, J. (1960–1961). *Le séminaire. Livre VIII. Le transfert.* Paris: Seuil, 1991.

Lacan, J. (1964). *Le séminaire. Livre XI. Les quatre concepts fondamentaux de la psychanalyse.* Paris: Seuil, 1973.

Lacan, J. (1966). *Ecrits,* Paris: Seuil.

Lacan, J. (1972–1973). *Le séminaire. Livre XX. Encore.* Paris: Seuil, 1975.

Laplanche, J. (1970). *Vie et mort en psychanalyse.* Paris: Flammarion.

Moscovici, M. (1980). Préface. L. Andreas-Salomé. *L'amour du narcissisme.* Paris: Gallimard.

Riviere, J. (1929). Womanliness as a masquerade. *International journal of psychoanalysis, 10*, 303–313.

Schaeffer, J. (2000). *Le refus du féminin.* Paris: PUF.

Winnicott, D.W. (1971. The split-off male and female elements to be found in men and women. In: *Playing and reality.* London: Tavistock Publications.

Woolf, V. (1981). *A writer's diary.* New York: Harcourt.

Woolf, V. (2001). *A room of one's own and three guineas.* London: Vintage.

8 The mother, trauma and writing

Writing and the mother

In the heart of the creation of two great women novelists, Virginia Woolf and Marguerite Duras, lies the suffering and the passion for the mother and writing becomes a means to accomplish the mourning of the object, hence to become liberated from the maternal imago. For Duras, writing corresponds to the colossal effort that she made in order to open the closed doors of her childhood and reach what seemed impenetrable to her. This effort was almost equivalent to a muscular force, as she was faced with "a mass between life and death' (my own translation) that she had to tear off from herself, break into pieces and shape (Duras, 1987, pp. 30–31). As a child, she used to witness her mother's desperation, which was brutal. In *The lover*, she writes: 'I had the luck to have a mother desperate with a despair so unalloyed that sometimes even life's happiness, at its most poignant, couldn't quite make her forget it' (Duras, 2006, p. 18). Both of her parents, who used to work as teachers in France, were attracted by the idea of going away to Indochina, after having read about Pierre Loti's adventures in colonial and oriental lands. The couple settled in Indochina and lived happily for a few years until the death of the father. The young widow had found herself, with her three young children, in great poverty. After numerous attempts, she obtained a piece of land that she intended to cultivate. But as she had not bribed the office of the land register, she was given land that could not be cultivated. The mother struggled to build a dam to protect her land against the huge tides of the Pacific Ocean so that she and her neighbours could cultivate it. But the dam was not able to resist the huge tides and every time succumbed to them. This blind and senseless struggle against nature lasted seven years, representing at the same time the mother's helplessness and desperation in the face of the cruel adversity of her life.

Marguerite Duras wrote about this experience in one of her first novels, *The sea wall* (1986). In contrast to this book, in the centre of which lies her mother's despair and the daughter's love for her, in *The lover* (2006) she

DOI: 10.4324/9781003232261-8

succeeds in putting into words both the love and hate for her mother that had been silenced till then.

> In the books I've written about my childhood I can't remember, suddenly, what I left out, what I said. I think I wrote about our love for our mother, but I don't know if I wrote about how we hated her too, or about our love for one another, and our terrible hatred too, in that common family history of ruin and death which was ours whatever happened, in love or in hate, and which I still can't understand however hard I try, which is still beyond my reach, hidden in the very depths of my flesh, blind as a new-born child. It's the area on whose brink silence begins. What happens there is silence, the slow travail of my whole life. I'm still there, watching those possessed children, as far away from the mystery now as I was then. I've never written, though I thought I wrote, never loved though I thought I loved, never done anything but wait outside the closed door.
>
> (Duras, 2006, p. 29)

In *The lover*, she writes about her impossible love for the mother and the Chinese lover that she had met at the age of fifteen. Her love for the Chinese lover was desperate because she knew that she would have to leave him and go to France in order to become a writer. On his part, the Chinese lover, who came from one of the wealthiest families in Saigon, knew also that his love for this young girl was hopeless. He had to be wed to a rich woman and have an heir, according to their tradition. So, both of them knew that their separation was inevitable and this impossibility marked their love and passion. In spite of having created *The lover* almost fifty years after having fallen in love with the Chinese lover, Duras still had while writing the feeling of this unfathomable and mute place of her childhood. Her suffering had not lost any of its intensity, nor the emotion of her first love, which was still warm. She had written it when she was around seventy years old. She created this novel from the ravages produced by her childhood as well as by those of her later life. She had written about the girl, the child, equally mad and brutal as her mother and her elder brother. Her mother's misery had permeated her childhood and there had been no possibility of dreaming and having illusions. There was no centre, no-body in the sense of an attentive presence and she had always been sad.

The rupture with her mother was produced when her young brother died in 1942. Duras had already left Saigon in 1931 with her mother and her young brother for France. She was eighteen years old then. Later her mother had returned to Saigon with her two sons. The urge to write became the means to tear herself from the moral and physical misery that had surrounded her childhood. Her first book was published a year after her young brother's death, for whose death she held responsible her elder brother, who was the only one that the mother designated as 'my child'. The mother defended him unconditionally in spite of his perversity. He had the soul of a killer, an impulse to kill, abuse others and make them suffer. The terror provoked by his violence had accompanied the misfortunes of their childhood. He had sowed so much fear in her young brother's heart that it had become weak and fragile and had not resisted the infection caused by pneumonia. She had received a telegram from Saigon announcing her younger brother's death – he was twenty-seven years old. The pain she experienced was so poignant and unbearable that she wanted to kill herself. She had recently lost a baby and she asked herself if the pain she felt was provoked by the loss of the baby. But then she thought that it could not be the pain of the baby that she had never met. This agony corresponded to the loss of her younger brother, who had been *her* child. Her love for her mother ended the day she received the telegram announcing her younger brother's death. She could not overcome the horror inspired by the pathological tie between her mother and her elder brother and ended by effacing both of them. The pain created oblivion of both of them but also that of her younger brother. In *The lover*, she brutally expresses the degree to which her hatred had led to the effacement of her mother's memory: 'She died, for me, of my younger brother's death'.

> In my head I no longer have the scent of her skin, nor in my eyes the colour of her eyes. I can't remember her voice, except sometimes when it grew soft with the weariness of evening. Her laughter I can't hear any more – neither her laughter nor her cries. It's over, I don't remember. That's why I can write about her so easily now, so long, so fully. She's become just something you write without difficulty, cursive writing.
>
> (Duras, 2006, p. 32)

The ravages of the relation between mother and daughter

Julia Kristeva dedicates to Duras the last chapter of *Black sun* (1992), as well as a chapter in *La haine et le pardon* (2005). In the latter she declares her complicity with the writer. Both Duras and herself had felt like strangers in France, Kristeva being born in Bulgaria and Duras in Indochina. They had brought their culture and language from their native countries. Kristeva situates precisely Duras' writing in the impossibility/possibility for a woman to overcome her hatred with regard to her mother. Duras had been saved thanks to her writing, which became an attempt to give shape to the formless mass of traces, intense affects and images with regard to the maternal object. Marie-Magdaleine Lessana (2000) refers to Lacan in order to discuss the tormentuous relationship between mother and daughter. Lacan (1973) examines the destructive aspects of the relationship between mother and daughter that he relates to the expectations *as a woman* that the young woman has of her mother. The daughter would demand from her mother 'something substantial' that could provide a basis for her female identity and would be disappointed by the impossibility of obtaining it. She would not make such a passionate claim to her father, as it is a demand from *woman to woman*. The weakest part of both Lacan's and Lessana's reflexions consists in envisaging the daughter's relation to the mother without taking into consideration her early attachment or what Kestemberg (1984), Godfrind (2001), Cournut-Janin (1988), Faure-Pragier (2011) and Denis (1992) call primary homosexuality. The question that we then ask is: At what stage would Lacan and Lessana situate the origin of the girl's demand? We know that a process is initiated from the moment the girl is born and even before that, during the mother's pregnancy. In our understanding, Lacan and Lessana situate the origin of the antagonism at the onset of puberty. The girl's hate with respect to the mother would be caused by the disappointment that she experiences in the absence of a mirror that can reflect how to become a woman. In other words, the mother would not provide her daughter a mirror of her femininity. Lessana (2000) underlines the division between the radical strangeness experienced by the girl with respect to her body and the alterity of the other woman's body, the mother, who is the object of desire. In the absence of a mirror, the daughter feels dispossessed of her own femininity, particularly when she faces the feminine image of her mother, who is desirable. She perceives her mother as a woman who does not provide the key to femininity in spite of possessing it, and therefore resents her. The daughter grows up facing the enigma of her mother as a woman who has sexuality. Then appears the troubling question: How does one become a woman? There would be no given answer to this. Each woman would have to build her own femininity and this is why there are different ways of building it, among which figure motherhood and sublimation. Motherhood is a possible route to building female identity and provides fulfilment as a woman, whereas sublimation as part of 'itineraries of desire' (Glocer Fiorini, 2019) becomes a means of liberation and fulfilment. In *Writing* (2011), Duras remarks that writing has always been for her 'a right to tell', an aspect that she considers to be totally ignored by women. In this sense, the urgency to write and the effort to articulate what a woman experiences in her inner world in relation with the external world, become something that shapes female subjectivity.

The ravishing by another woman

Lessana (2000) and Kristeva (1992) consider that the only issue that the daughter can find to the hostile relation with the mother consists in an aggressive confrontation that can allow detachment from her. However, the impossibility of undergoing this trial indicates the degree to which a woman can be captured by the maternal imago, leading to a lack of consistency that entails the risk of being ravished by another woman. This impossibility lies in the centre of Duras' novel *The ravishing of Lol V. Stein* (1966), which is one of her most enigmatic novels. Lol had not been able to face the hostility with respect to the mother and had remained 'her mother's child' who had to be protected and guided. It was only after having married and moved away from her native town that she was capable of expressing her hate with regard to her mother. The novel opens with a ball that takes place every summer in the casino of S. Thala. Lola Stein, nineteen years old, and her fiancé Michael Richardson attend the ball. During the event she painfully witnesses her fiancé's desire for a beautiful woman, mature in age and dressed in black. She is dazzled by her image and swept away by the spectacle of her fiancé, who is possessed with this mature woman. She is incapable of reacting to this situation and expresses her pain and anger. The omission of herself to the point of effacement drives her insane. She understands 'too well' that her fiancé has chosen the other woman and she adheres passively to it. The fiancé even asks for Lol's approval in order to leave the ball with the other woman and she gives her acquiescence. It is Lol's mother who brutally reacts to what has happened and insults the couple, accusing them of having harmed 'her child'. It is only then that Lol is able to cry, freeing herself from the paralysis in which she had found herself. She tries to retain the couple, is confused, uttering senseless things to them and faints when she sees them leaving the ball. In the following days and weeks she collapses, feeling hopeless and completely overwhelmed with extenuation and suffering. But it is a suffering that has no subject, as she is not aware of her own suffering and is absent from herself. She begins to identify herself by the name of Lol V. Stein, instead of Lola Stein or Lola Valérie Stein, which are her real names. The name that she has invented, notes Lessana (2000), becomes the symbol of her ravishing by the other woman, as she can no more recognize herself in her own name. Lol had been swept away by the scene of her fiancé, ravished by the other woman, and she witnessed it without being able to react to it. In her perplexity, an idea had passed through her mind that there would be a key word that could provide an identity for her, thanks to which she would name the experience she had undergone. But she could not find the word, instead *there was a hole in its place. 'It was an absence-word, a hole-word, whose centre would have* been hollowed out into a hole, the kind of hole in which all other words would have been buried' (Duras, 1966, p. 38).

> Replaced by that woman, unto her very breath. Lol holds her breath as this woman's body appears to this man, her own fades, fades, voluptuous pleasure, from the world. 'You. You alone'. Lol had never been able to carry this divesting of Anne-Marie Stretter's dress in slow-motion, this velvet annihilation of her own person, to its conclusion.
> (Duras, 1966, p. 40)

In this sense Lol's self-annihilation is shocking for us. Lessana points to Duras' devilish elaboration of Lol's character, impossible to grasp: 'Lol embodies a point of extreme subjectivity, shocking and unheard' (Lessana, 2000, p. 263, my own translation). In a tribute rendered to Duras and organized by the periodical *Cahiers Renaud-Barrault* (1965), Lacan reflects on the ravishing of Lol. He speaks in a touching way about this young girl of nineteen years old, in love and arriving at the ball with all her illusions till the moment she witnesses her fiancé falling in love with the other woman. She is 'stripped' of her lover as if she had been stripped of her dress and there is nothing left behind of her innocence and the splendour of her body. Lacan underlines the other's role in the constitution of the body image, who 'dresses', 'redresses' or 'undresses' the subject. In other words, he refers to the mirror stage in which the mother identifies and recognizes her child. It is owing to her gaze and love that the daughter's body image can be 'dressed' but with the condition that a process of differentiation is inaugurated between mother and daughter and this was not Lol's case.

The comedy of the mascarade

As we have seen with Marguerite Duras, creation becomes the means to overcome the melancholic grief with regard to the maternal object and writing becomes equivalent to the act of matricide. In spite of placing the woman in the centre of a book on women and melancholia, Anne Juranville (1993) defends the idea that women would have an advantage with respect to men to the extent that they are less prone to melancholia. Thanks to the 'comedy of the mascarade', a woman would deliver herself more easily from the maternal imago and traverse more easily the mourning of the object. It is by means of 'the comedy of the mascarade' that the woman would become the object of desire of the other. The display of the mascarade concerns the surface of her body, onto which can be projected the internal processes. This mode of externalization would protect the female subject from the threat of deepening that characterizes melancholia. However, the division that operates between a woman's presentation with respect to the gaze of the other and her being constitutes a source of fragility and vulnerability. 'It is her existence that she puts into play in this "imaginary partition" constitutive of her identity' (Juranville, 1993, p. 178, my on translation). How is it that women would have an advantage over men if they present themselves to others by means of an imaginary construction, a source of vulnerability in them? Thanks to the function of the mascarade, women would disguise their castration. Dresses and accessories covering their body would serve to give a sense of phallic completeness. But, the imaginary construction of the phallic completeness of the body requires recognition on the part of the other. In her relation with the male lover, the woman is particularly vulnerable to his gaze and desire. The loss of the lover signifies the loss of recognition from the part of the object, that which plunges her into depression and melancholia. Hence, the quest for recognition on the part of the lover is the Achilles heel of a woman.

We consider that Juranville's (1993) conception is important in a negative sense because it shows the defects of a theoretical thinking that does not take into consideration the feminine and the psychic elements of interiority. Her thinking serves to demonstrate the limits of a phallocentric conception of female identity and it would be more precisely appropriate to speak of 'the refusal of the feminine' (Schaeffer, 2000). What draws our attention in Juranville's theory is its essentialist aspect. After having depicted an abstract picture of the 'essence' of women, she notes that this picture has been brought into question by the historical upheavals that have shaken the very basis of female identity. If this is so, why would she defend 'the comedy of the mascarade' as the paradigm of female identity? Juranville's position is paradoxical when she accords special attention to Virginia Woolf and Antigone, as creators. She makes a distinction between creation and sublimation, the first being the privilege of women who have transgressed the limits established by the social and cultural order. In this sense, she establishes a hierarchy of values, creation being placed at a higher place than sublimation. Antigone would be the paradigm of the woman who enters into the scene of history after having transgressed the cultural order. Juranville remarks that the western world has produced a rupture in women's identity, 'offering her melancholia as well as liberation' (Juranville, 1993, p. 245, my own translation). In other words, melancholia would be the price of her liberation but this affirmation does not modify her conception with respect to female identity; melancholia, as a defiance to the Other and spirituality are reserved for men (Juranville, 1993).

The only sublimation that Juranville can recognize is maternal love but even that would be limited in its scope, as she thinks that it is not appropriated by women. We find in Juranville's approach to sublimation the old prejudices of the Freudian conception. Thanks to the logic of the mascarade, women would encounter 'a resistance to overcome the immanence and the freedom that requires spiritual work' (Juranville, 1993, p. 242, my own translation). In Freudian theory, women are not capable of sublimation because they do not experience a castration anxiety that can precipitate the radical resolution of the Oedipus complex and the formation of a strong super-ego. The castration anxiety would be the cause of men's participation in cultural productions and development of spiritual work. Freud establishes a relation between the woman's weak position in society and the absence of a strict and stable super-ego that would be independent of its affective roots. However, Juranville's (1993) study has the merit of according a central place to sublimation to the degree of conceiving it, along with neurosis and perversion, as an existential structure that is opposed to psychosis. Sublimation as an existential structure would protect the subject against psychosis. However, the lives of great creators, such as Van Gogh, Virginia Woolf, Camille Claudel, Antonin Artaud and others, have not been exempt from agonies, breakdowns, madness or suicide. But their genius work has conferred on them the utmost possibility of a subjective realization and expression. Evelyn Séchaud (2005) underlines the close relation between trauma, mourning and creation, as illustrated by the propositions of Michel de M'Uzan (1977) and André Green (1992). The latter remarks that there is always a narcissistic injury, a loss at the origin of 'the work of writing'. Green conceives writing as a *work* whose product would be a literary creation, through which the traumatic has been transformed. Marguerite Duras' and Virginia Woolf's literary creations illustrate the relation between mourning and writing. Séchaud remarks that the mourning of the object provokes a crisis, an internal upheaval, in a process in which the loss 'enters in resonance with anterior losses of all kinds: deaths, certainly, but also renunciations, ruptures, separations, which have left their traces – traces of suffering, injury always ready to be reopened' (2005, p. 1320, my own translation). However, thanks to the effects of *après-coup*, the possibility of symbolization and transformation of the traumatic arises. Hence, an analogy can be established between the work of mourning as Freud (1917e) defined it in 'Mourning and melancholia', and the work of sublimation as the creative process that presupposes a psychic work, a psychic elaboration with respect to the loss.

Trauma and sublimation

Thanks to Virginia Woolf's autobiographical texts, edited by Jeanne Schulkind and gathered in *Moments of being* (1985b), we learn about her childhood and adolescence, which had been particularly difficult. Her mother's loss had been the major trauma that had marked these years. We can establish a relation between the traumatic loss of the mother and her writing. In this sense, the Freudian argument about a special disposition existing 'from the very beginning' would not be sufficient to explain Woolf's extraordinary capacity to create. On the contrary, she identifies the traumatic events that she had experienced as the source of her urge to write. In 'A sketch of the past' (1985b), one of the memoirs written in full maturity, she establishes a relation between the psychological shocks that she had received in her adolescence and her writing. Two major traumas had occurred during that time. She was thirteen years old when she lost her mother and fifteen years old when her eldest sister Stella died. She felt that these shocks had provoked the urgent need to explain and elaborate the essence of things that she named as 'moments of being'. However, her losses were not limited to these two major events. She was twenty-two years old when her father died from cancer and two years later her brother Thoby died from a typhoid fever.

In 'Reminiscences', the first memoir written in her years of apprenticeship, Woolf narrates how she was struck by her mother's death. An inconsolable grief reigned in the house: 'for surely there was something in the darkened rooms, the groans, the passionate lamentations that passed the normal limits of sorrow' (Woolf, 1985a, p. 40). She describes the chronic state of confusion in which the children had found themselves in this atmosphere.

> We were quite naturally unhappy; feeling a definite need, that was recognizable pain, and the sharp pang grew to be almost welcome in the midst of the sultry and opaque life which was not felt, had nothing real in it, and yet swam about us, and choked us and blinded us.
>
> (Woolf, 1985a, p. 45)

On one hand, an idealized image of the mother, and on the other, the never-ending grievances and lamentations of the father, relatives and parents' friends, impeded the children from referring to a human being who had died and had to be mourned.

> we had but a dull sense of gloom which could not honestly be referred to the dead; unfortunately it did not quicken our feeling for the living; but hideous as it was, obscured both living and dead; and for long did unpardonable mischief by substituting for the shape of a true and most vivid mother, nothing better than an unlovable phantom.
>
> (Woolf, 1985a, p. 45)

Her mother was the centre of the house, in charge of her eight children, her husband and the numerous guests that used to visit them and sometimes stay with them. Julia Jackson, at the age of 24, had lost her first husband Herbert Duckworth and as a widow already had the responsibility of her three children, George, Stella and Gerald. Several years later she got married to Leslie Stephen, with whom she procreated Thoby, Vanessa, Virginia and Adrian. She had also to take care of Laura, who was Leslie Stephen's daughter from his first marriage. Virginia describes Laura as mentally deficient but her troublesome behaviour in her childhood suggests that she was psychotic. Julia took care not only of her eight children, but also of her mother, her sister, friends and the sick people. Virginia remarks that in such a crowded and busy house, it was hard to capture her mother's individualized attention. Her mother was 'a general presence rather than a particular person to a child of seven or eight' (Woolf, 1985, p. 84).

Woolf's first breakdown occurred after her mother's death at the age of thirteen and the second after her father's death at the age of twenty-two. Her mother's death, however, was unthinkable and desperate. She was for a long time obsessed by her death, hearing her voice and seeing her in the house as if she continued to live. It was only with the publication of her novel *To the lighthouse* (1981c), thirty-two years after her loss that she felt liberated from her. At the age of thirteen, her mother's loss had been a blow of such a magnitude that it was impossible to mourn it. Two years later, her elder sister Stella's death reactivated the grief of her mother's loss. She notes how the father and the children were haunted by the mother's and Stella's ghosts. 'But Stella's death two years later fell on a different substance; a mind stuff and being stuff that was extraordinarily unprotected, unformed, unshielded, apprehensive, receptive, anticipatory' (1985, p. 124). After her mother's death, Stella had taken over her mother's role, trying very hard to maintain the family together and look after her stepfather. After his wife's death, Lesley Stephen was more tyrannical than ever in his exigencies and necessities and in this way tried to absorb Stella's attention and care. The second blow provoked by Stella's death led Virginia to envisage, despite the sense of a catastrophe, that things could not continue in this way and that she should do something for herself. She discovered that it was her 'shock-receiving capacity' that made her a writer. These shocks became the urgent cause of the need for explanation and elaboration of the essence of things. Thanks to her writing, she could exorcize her mother's death and be liberated from her ghostly presence. The writing of *To the lighthouse* is situated between 'Reminiscences' and 'A sketch of the past'. While in the first memoir her mother is depicted as a respected, idealized but a distant figure, in the second she is treated more realistically and in a more ambivalent way. Equally her feelings with regard to her father undergo a transformation, changing from the resentment that she had experienced after Stella's death to a better understanding of him. She had held him responsible for Stella's death because of his tyrannical and possessive behaviour, particularly when Stella wished to get married to Jack Hills. She confesses that her reading of Freud had permitted her to acknowledge her love and passion for her father. Contrary to her early memoir 'Reminiscences' that is marked by her mother's loss, in *A writer's diary* (1981a) Woolf attributes her feelings of great pain to the losses of both parents, expressing that the writing of *To the lighthouse* had allowed her to overcome the grief of both losses. 'I used to think of him and mother daily; but writing *To the lighthouse* laid them in my mind [...] and writing of them was a necessary act' (Woolf, 1981c p. 135). In fact, she considers that it was in this novel that she had 'deepened most'.

In *To the lighthouse*, Woolf lends to Mrs Ramsay some characteristics of her mother that she used to resent but also her complexity and depth. Mrs Ramsay has a vital presence in the family. However, in spite of depicting her as a woman dedicated to the well-being of her family in oblivion of herself, she equally pictures her as a person who is capable of capturing intense moments of being. There is a moving passage in the novel where we can feel Mrs Ramsay more intimately. She has finished her daily labours, it is nighttime and she can finally be herself in a moment of retreat.

> For now she need not think about anybody. She could be herself, by herself. And that was what now she often felt the need of-to think; well, not even to think. To be silent; to be alone. All the being and the doing, expansive, glittering, vocal, evaporated; and one shrunk, with a sense of solemnity, to being oneself, a wedge-shaped core of darkness, something invisible to others.
>
> (Woolf 1981b, p. 62)

In the novel Mrs Ramsay, like her mother, dies at an early age. Hermione Lee (1996) underlines the abruptness with which Woolf announces Mrs Ramsay's death, which is in contrast to the never-ending sorrow and grief of her father as well as of the household when her mother had died. In the novel, it is to Lily Briscoe, a painter, that Woolf lends her feelings. 'What was the problem then? She must try to get hold of something that evaded her. It evaded her when she thought of Mrs. Ramsay'. In a similar way to Lily, who could not identify her feelings about Mrs Ramsay, Woolf could not define her feelings with regard to her own mother. In 'A sketch of the past' (1985b), she attributes it to the non-existence of moments shared with her. She never remembered being alone with her, as there was always somebody who came to interrupt them. It is a paradox that she could not grieve her mother's death when her father's lamentations invaded the house. Lee accounts for this paradox by referring to the father's 'extortionate, melodramatic grief'. She notes: 'If the daughter could not feel enough, that was partly because the father felt too much' (Lee, 1996, p. 131).

In 'A sketch of the past', Woolf (1985b) has the opportunity to reflect on the traumatic moments of her childhood and adolescence that had produced a sense of horror and despair and had led to a physical collapse. As she got older, she considered that her capacity to provide an explanation for them blunted the pain, 'the sledge-hammer force of the blow' (p. 72). Being able to explain them gave her the opportunity to transform them, whereas in the past she had perceived them as blows coming 'from an enemy behind the cotton wool of daily life' (p. 72), against which she could not react. In this sense, the capacity to transform the painful events through her writing made her feel real and became the occasion of a spiritual revelation that created an intense emotional experience.

> I make it real by putting into words. It is only by putting it into words that I make it whole; this wholeness means that it has lost its power to hurt me; it gives me, perhaps because by doing so I take away the pain, a great delight to put the severed parts together. Perhaps this is the strongest pleasure known to me. It is the rapture I get in when in writing I seem to discover what belongs to what, making a scene come right; making a character come together. From this I reach what I might call a philosophy; at any rate it is a constant idea of mine; that behind the cotton wool is hidden a pattern; that we – I mean all

human beings – are connected with this; that the whole world is a work of art; that we are parts of the work of art.

(1985b, p. 72)

In *A writer's diary*, Woolf expresses that writing makes her plunge into the depths and richness of her mind: 'I can write and write and write now: the happiest feeling in the world' (Woolf, 1981a, p. 68). However, plunging into the depths of the mind is perilous and is associated with death. In her 'Foreword' to *Mrs Dalloway* (1981b), Maureen Howard (1981) remarks that Woolf as a modernist writer had broken with the tradition of the classical novel and this enterprise had its risks. In fact, Woolf had not only broken with the tradition of the classical novel but also with the values and mentalities of Victorian society, represented by her father and her elder brothers, George and Gerald Duckworth. By transgressing their patriarchal values, she had become a feminist. However, the ecstatic and vital experience of writing has its price, as it equally had for Marguerite Duras. In *Writing* (2011), Duras expresses that solitude produces the necessary and inviolable space of creation, but it is 'a suicide'. The price for having dared to come out and scream is very costly. In this sense, for both Woolf and Duras, writing becomes a transgression of the social and cultural order that causes 'both melancholia and liberation' (Juranville, 1993).

References

Cournut-Janin, M. (1998). *Féminin et féminité*, Paris: PUF.

Denis, P. (1982). Homosexualité primaire, base de contradiction. *Revue française de psychanalyse*, 46:1, 35–42.

De M'Uzan, M. (1977). *De l'art à la mort*. Paris: Gallimard.

Duras, M. (1966). *The ravishing of Lol Stein*. New York: Pantheon Books.

Duras, M (1986). *The sea wall*. New York: Farrar, Straus & Giroux.

Duras, M. (1987). *La vie matérielle*. Paris: Gallimard.

Duras, M. (2006). *The lover*. London: Harper Collins.

Duras, M. (2011). *Writing*. Minnesota: University of Minnesota Press.

Faure-Pragier, S. (2011). Rester psychanalyste face au chaos des nouvelles filiations. *Revue française de psychanalyse*, 75:4, 1063–1080.

Freud, S. (1917e). Mourning and melancholia. *SE, 14*: 243–258.

Freud, S. (1925j). Some psychical consequences of the anatomical distinction between the sexes. *SE, 19*: 243–258.

Glocer-Fiorini, L. (2019). La deconstruction du 'féminin': discours, logiques et pouvoir. Les implications théorico-cliniques. *Revue française de psychanalyse, 83:3*, 825–839.

Godfrind, J. (2001). *Comment la féminité vient aux femmes*. Paris: PUF.

Green, A. (1992). *La déliason*. Paris: Les Belles Lettres.

Howard, M. (1981). Foreword. V. Woolf, *Mrs. Dalloway*. New York: Harcourt.

Juranville, A. (1993). *La femme et la mélancolie*. Paris: PUF.

Kestemberg, E. (1984). 'Astride' ou homosexualité, identité, adolescence. Quelques propositions hypothétiques. *Les cahiers du Centre de Psychanalyse et de Psychothérapie*, no. 8.

Kristeva, J. (1992). *Black sun: Depression and melancholia*. New York: Columbia University Press.

Kristeva, J. (2005). *La haine et le pardon*. Paris: Fayard.

Lacan, J. (1965). Hommage fait à Marguerite Duras, du ravissement de Lol V. Stein. *Cahiers Renaud-Barrault*. Paris: Julliard.

Lacan, J. (1973). L'étourdit. *Scilicet*, 4, 5–52.

Lee, H. (1996). *Virginia Woolf*. London: Vintage.

Lessana, M.-M. (2000). *Entre mère et fille: Un ravage*. Paris: Hachette.

Schaeffer, J. (2000). *Le refus du féminin*. Paris: PUF, p. 15.

Séchaud, E. (2005). Perdre, sublimer. *Revue française de psychanalyse*, 69:5, 1309–1380.

Woolf, V. (1981a). *A writer's diary*. New York: Harcourt.

Woolf, V. (1981b). *Mrs. Dalloway*. New York: Harcourt.

Woolf, V. (1981c). *To the lighthouse*. New York: Harcourt.

Woolf, V. (1985a). Reminiscences. In: J. Schulkind (Ed.), *Moments of being*. New York: Harcourt.

Woolf, V. (1985b). A sketch of the past. In: J. Schulkind (Ed.), *Moments of being*. New York: Harcourt.

9 The sexual and sublimation

Trauma and sublimation

As we have seen with Virginia Woolf and Marguerite Duras, writing becomes a means to overcome the trauma. In his seminar *La sublimation*, Laplanche (1998) examines sublimation in relation with trauma, placing the sexual drive in the centre of the human being's capacity to transform even the most traumatic events. A century before, in 'Civilized' sexual morality' (1908d), Freud had already inaugurated his reflexion on sublimation and its powerful effects at the service of civilization.

> It places extraordinarily large amounts of force at the disposal of civilized activity, and it does this in virtue of its especially marked characteristic of being able to displace its aim without materially diminishing its intensity. This capacity to exchange its originally sexual aim for another one, which is no longer sexual but which is psychically related to the first aim, is called the capacity for *sublimation*.
>
> (1908d, p. 187, original emphasis)

Laplanche parts from the Freudian idea of the high plasticity of the sexual drive and remarks that the human being has the capacity to create the non-sexual incessantly and close to the original sexual aim. The non-sexual refers to artistic, literary and intellectual productions at the service of society, which are, however, psychically related to the original sexual aim, which is the satisfaction of the drive. What is striking in the satisfaction characterizing sublimation is that the drive operates its displacement from the original sexual aim to objects socially valorized without losing any of its intensity. The investment of 'extraordinarily large amounts of force' (Freud, 1908d, p. 187) at the service of cultural acquisitions is an indicator of the intensity of satisfaction inherent to sublimation. Even when it is a question of trauma, its transformation and the possibility of creating something *new* from it has in its origin the *sexual*, which concerns infantile sexuality that is polymorphic and multiple. The instinct as a vital function is perverted by the search for pleasure, whose origin is infantile.

DOI: 10.4324/9781003232261-9

Hence, sublimation is 'a kind of a *neo-genesis of sexuality*' (Laplanche, 1988, emphasis in original) consisting in the re-invention, re-creation of sexuality from all kinds of external disturbances including the traumatic. At the termination of analysis, the creation of new psychic forms by the analysand is also a sublimation to the extent that these forms imply psychic transformations leading to a new way of experiencing oneself and life. The creation of these forms as well as the artistic and intellectual productions lean on the *sexual*; whilst 'the transference of the transference' (Laplanche, 1987) is an indicator that the analysand has been capable of displacing the transference love to another object, which becomes the object of sublimation. In fact, transference can never be 'liquidated' but can only at the end of a fruitful analytical work be displaced to another object that will be libidinally invested.

Lacan and Laplanche concur in the paradoxical nature of satisfaction in sublimation. Despite the derivation of the sexual aim to a non-sexual aim, there is no loss in the intensity of satisfaction. In his seminar *L'éthique de la psychanalyse* (1959–1960), Lacan draws our attention to the enigmatic nature of the satisfaction in sublimation. While the natural aim of the drive corresponds to the obtention of satisfaction by means of the return of the repressed, sublimation is a *direct* mode of satisfaction of the drive without undergoing repression. In *Leonardo da Vinci and a memory of his childhood* (1910c), Freud expresses that the libido can be sublimated into curiosity as well as into the urge for research, without undergoing repression. Hence, sublimation reveals the high plasticity of the drive, as opposed to the notion of instinct. That is why Lacan remarks that sublimation reveals the true nature of the drive. In a similar way, Laplanche is also clear about the fact that sublimation can never involve the instinct. He returns to the Freudian concept of 'anaclisis' to examine the relation between the non-sexual and the sexual. If the question of desire is central in psychoanalytic practice, it is because sexuality is not the expression of the instinct but that of the drive.

In *Life and death in psychoanalysis* (1985), Laplanche remarks that sexuality represents the model of the drive, but with the condition of envisaging it as a deviation from the instinct not only conceptually but also on a real basis. The genesis of the sexual drive is realized by its derivation from the satisfaction of the *infant's* necessities, as the Freudian concept of anaclisis illustrates. The genesis of sexuality is due to its derivation from the biological to the psychic. So, sexuality, which at the beginning leans on a vital function, becomes dissociated from it. The prototype of oral satisfaction is not the sucking at the mother's breast but sensual sucking of a part of the body, which provides an auto-erotic satisfaction. Laplanche (1985) takes the measure of the concept of auto-eroticism by emphasizing that it is situated at time two. Time one corresponds to anaclisis from which sexual pleasure derives. The loss of the (partial) object of the vital function, the breast, takes place precisely at the moment when the total object, the mother, can be represented by the child. It is the milk, the real object of the vital function that is lost, whereas the breast, by means of auto-eroticism, becomes the fantasized breast. The latter is the object of the sexual drive to the extent that sexuality does not have a real object. The sexual object is displaced with regard to the object of the vital function, in *contiguity* from milk to the breast as its symbol. In *Three essays*, Freud's formulation 'The finding of an object is in fact a refinding of it' (1905d, p. 222) signifies that the object to be refound is never the object of a vital function, but its substitute. What is sought consists in an object that is displaced with regard to the object of the hallucinated satisfaction. This impossibility marks the quest of the object and situates it precisely in the orbit of desire, an aspect that goes precisely into the heart of Lacan's conception of object *a* that we will discuss in the next chapter.

Leonardo da Vinci and the traumatic

Laplanche (1998) examines the question of trauma in Leonardo by referring to Eissler's book *Leonardo da Vinci: Psychoanalytic notes on the enigma* (1961), as well as to an article by Lowenfeld 'Psychic trauma and productive experience in the artist' (1941). What he finds notable in Lowenfeld's paper is that the essential in the artistic creation does not consist in the origin of the talent but in *the source of the forces that led to the sublimation*. These forces originate, in the case of Leonardo da Vinci, as well as in Virginia Woolf and Marguerite Duras, in traumatic forces. Lowenfeld (1941)remarks that the artist is constantly occupied by the attempt to gain control over an excessive amount of external stimuli. The traumatic is here visualized as originating in the external world despite the subject perceiving it as inside at the same time. Michel de M'Uzan (1977) remarks the presence of the traumatic experience at the origin of the creative process. The traumatic consists of the irruption of the real in the form of something that cannot be represented and symbolized. Hence, creation becomes the means to master and elaborate these painful experiences. Eissler (1961) approaches this in a similar way to Lowenfeld (1941), when he posits that Leonardo was extremely vulnerable to external stimuli that provoked affects of terror and helplessness in him. In addition to external stimuli that had become overwhelming for Leonardo, he also suffered from psychic trauma. He was separated from his mother at a young age and raised by his father and his wife. After this separation he never met his mother again. Laplanche (1998), who comments on Eissler's conception of trauma, observes that the model of trauma becomes here a model of defence against it, allowing its elaboration and symbolization. So, sublimation would be the fruit of a work of elaboration and symbolization of the trauma.

In *Leonardo da Vinci and a memory of his childhood* (1910c), Freud defines Leonardo's passion for knowledge and his intellectual investigation as an authentic sublimation, in opposition to his painting that seemed more

easily to activate his affects. It is a paradox that the extraordinary creativity and aesthetical quality of his painting are not considered as sublimation by Freud. Hence, in the Freudian perspective, an extraordinary
creativity as reflected by Leonardo's painting would have to include a
mental organization that allows sufficiently good psychic functioning.
Authentic sublimation would concern a psychical organization that could
assure the warding off of intense suffering. While Lowenfeld conceives a
successful sublimation as a defence against trauma, Freud does not take
into consideration the traumatic factor and sustains instead the presence
of a 'special disposition' existing from an early age. In 'Civilized' Sexual
Morality', he notes:

> It seems to us that it is the innate constitution of each individual
> which decides in the first instance how large a part of his sexual
> instinct it will be possible to sublimate and make use of. In addition
> to this, the effects of experience and the intellectual influences upon
> his mental apparatus succeed in bringing about the sublimation of a
> further portion of it.
>
> (1908d, p. 188)

On the other hand, Freud envisages analytical treatment as a means to
bring about sublimation in the patient, but this aspiration would not apply
to all of them. In 'Recommendations to physicians on analytic technique',
he precises:

> Not every neurotic has a high talent for sublimation; one can assume of
> many of them that they would not have fallen ill at all if they had pos-
> sessed the art of sublimating their instincts. If we press them unduly
> towards sublimation and cut them off from the most accessible and
> convenient instinctual satisfactions, we shall usually make life even
> harder for them than they feel it in any case [...] It must further be
> borne in mind that many people fall ill precisely from an attempt to
> sublimate their instincts beyond the degree permitted by their organ-
> ization and that in those who have a capacity for sublimation the pro-
> cess usually takes place of itself as soon as their inhibitions have been
> overcome by analysis.
>
> (1912e, p. 119)

In the neurotic, the repression of infantile curiosity constitutes an obstacle
for sublimation. If the patient can overcome his or her inhibitions during analysis, then there is a chance for sublimation. In *Leonardo da Vinci
and a memory of his childhood* (1910c), Freud describes three possible vicissitudes of infantile curiosity. In the first one, infantile curiosity succumbs
to repression. In the second one, as a result of sexual repression, 'the sup-
pressed sexual activities of research return from the unconscious in the

form of compulsive brooding' (1910c, p. 80). This process sexualizes think-ing itself, which is typical of obsessive neurosis. The third one, charac-terized by 'a special disposition', is 'the rarest and most perfect' type and exists out of the realm of neurosis.

> Instead, the libido evades the fate of repression by being sublimated from the very beginning into curiosity and by becoming attached to the powerful instinct for research as a reinforcement. Here, too, the research becomes to some extent compulsive and a substitute for sexual activity; but owing to the complete difference in the underly-ing psychical processes (sublimation instead of an irruption from the unconscious) the quality of neurosis is absent.
>
> (1910c, p. 80)

Hence, sublimation becomes 'from the very beginning' a vicissitude for the sexual drive. Laplanche (1998) defines the idea 'from the very begin-ning' as the moment of the first apparition of sexual excitement that can be transformed into curiosity. Baldacci (2005) remarks that sublimation 'from the very beginning' consists in the qualitative transformation of the drive, which involves the capacity to renounce its direct satisfaction, thanks to the plasticity of the drive. Hence, sublimation can meet the demands of the ego without involving repression. Freud establishes an opposition between sublimation and idealization. In 'On Narcissism: An introduc-tion' (1914c), he remarks that idealization corresponds to the exaltation and aggrandizement of the object without altering its nature. 'In so far as sublimation describes something that has to do with the instinct and idealization something to do with the object, the two concepts are to be distinguished from each other' (1914c, p. 94). By means of the aggrandize-ment of the object, the formation of the ideal causes an increase in the exigencies of the ego, which are erected as obstacles to the satisfaction of the drive. The formation of the ideal 'is the most powerful factor favour-ing repression', whereas sublimation concerns the satisfaction of the drive without involving repression. Hence, sublimation provokes effects on the growth and expansion of the ego, which are returned to as joy of life, sen-suality, love and eroticism.

The vicissitudes of the sexual drive at puberty

Bernard Penot (2001) examines the vicissitudes of the sexual drive in the period of latency and establishes an analogy between the psychic func-tioning in this period and sublimation. The period of latency concerns the suspension of the direct satisfaction of the sexual drive till the onset of puberty, whereas sublimation consists in the capacity to differ satisfaction at the service of the creation of socially valorized objects. In fact, the period of latency becomes a decisive time for the realization of sublimation. In his long psychoanalytic experience with adolescents in the context of a day-hospital, Penot (2001) focuses on the vicissitudes of the investments of the period of latency in order to ascertain if, at the onset of puberty, they have resisted or been wiped out by the warming brought about by the sexual drive. This evaluation permits him to see whether sublimations in the period of latency have been authentic or if they have been just simply reactive formations. The capacity to sustain the tension inherent in desire that Penot names as 'passivation', which is a neologism, concerns the capacity to be subjected to the drive allowing oneself to be carried along by it. It is the parental encouragement of the child's accomplishments and not their repression that supports and favours the realization of sublimations. In this perspective, Penot distinguishes between the repressive parental super-ego and the ego ideal transmitted via the introjection of certain qualities of the parents' responses that are perceived from an early age. The child perceives the signs of the parental *jouissance* resulting from a certain know-how with respect to reality. In this sense, the ego ideal transmitted by the parents refers to a certain aspect of knowing how to take pleasure.

References

Baldacci, J.L. (2005). 'Dès le début'... la sublimation? *Revue française de psychanalyse, 69*: 5, 1405–1474.

De M'Uzan, M. & Pontalis, J.-B. (1977). Ecrire, psychanalyser, écrire. Echange de vues. *Nouvelle revue de psychanalyse, 16*, 5–26.

Eissler, K. (1961). *Leonardo da Vinci: Psychoanalytic notes on the enigma*. New York: International Universities Press.

Freud, S. (1905d). *Three essays on the theory of sexuality. SE, 7*: 130–243.

Freud, S. (1908d). 'Civilized' sexual morality and modern nervous illness. *SE, 9*: 181–204.

Freud, S. (1910c). *Leonardo da Vinci and a memory of his childhood. SE, 11*: 63–137.

Freud, S. (1912e). Recommendations to physicians practising psychoanalysis. *SE, 12*: 111–120.

Freud, S. (1914c). On narcissism: An introduction. *SE, 14*: 73–102.

Lacan, J. (1959–1960). *Le séminaire. Livre VII. L'éthique de la psychanalyse*. Paris: Seuil, 1986.

Laplanche, J. (1987). *Nouveaux fondements pour la psychanalyse*. Paris: PUF, p. 160.

Laplanche, J. (1998[1980]). *La sublimation*. Paris: PUF.

Laplanche, J. (1985). *Life and death in psychoanalysis*. Baltimore, MD: Johns Hopkins University Press.

Lowenfeld, H. (1941). Psychic trauma and productive experience in the artist. *Psychoanalytic quarterly, X*, 665–678.

Penot, B. (2001). *La passion du sujet freudien*. Paris: Erès.

10 The object in Lacan and in Winnicott

Object *a*

In his seminar *L'éthique de la psychanalyse* (1986), Lacan examines *Das Ding*, the German term for *Thing*, which is the primordial object. This term appears for the first time in Freud, in *Project for a scientific psychology* (1950[1895]). The traces and the bodily inscriptions left by the prehistoric object become the cause of the representations governed by the pleasure principle. Lacan follows the paths of Freud's thought, noting that the prehistoric object can never be forgotten. It is apprehended as something strange and as the first exteriority despite it being experienced inside the subject. In other words, at the origin something that is inside is projected outside. In 'Negation', Freud puts:

> It is now no longer a question of whether what has been perceived (a thing) shall be taken into the ego or not, but of whether something which is in the ego as a presentation can be re-discovered in perception (reality) as well. It is, we see, once more a question of *external* and *internal*. What is unreal, merely a presentation and subjective, is only internal; what is real is also there *outside*.
>
> (1925h, p. 237, emphasis in original)

The original experience of reality is divided between the dark nucleus of our being which lacks any possibility of signification and the movement of representations gravitating around this dark nucleus. Lacan coincides with Freud with respect to the primitive organization of reality. Freud communicates his point of view to Wilhelm Fliess, in his letter, no. 52, of December 6, 1896 (Masson, 1985). He remarks that the subject's primitive impression of the external world is situated outside the realm of signification, presenting itself not simply as a mark but especially as a transcription, a writing. The Freudian idea of a transcription approaches Lacan's conception of *Das Ding* as traces, inscriptions left from the prehistorical object. Hence, object *a* is the object that causes desire and is created in the traces of the lost partial objects, such as the breast, the faeces, the phallus,

DOI: 10.4324/9781003232261-10

the voice and the gaze. These objects, which represent the narcissistic union with the mother, become the remains of her body after having been subjected to primary symbolization, that is to primal repression. They are characterized by the possibility whereas for Melanie Klein (1932) the mythical body of the mother can be fantasized and is effectively the treasure of the child's fantasies. Thanks to this treasure, the child can establish imaginary equivalences between the objects fantasized inside the maternal body, such as the babies, the faeces, the penis, and the external objects. Hence, in the Kleinian conception this process leads to symbol-formation, which is a condition of sublimation.

Lacan's (1986) discussion on sublimation focuses on the subject's quest of *Das Ding*, which can never be found except for its 'coordinates of pleasure' and only in their regressive forms, relating to a time when satisfaction was hallucinatory. The primordial object can never be found again, as it is the object from which the infant was weaned. A basic tension, a discordance underlies the repetitive search of the object because it never coincides with the hallucinated one. It is in the name of the pleasure principle that the hallucinated object will be sought and never found. The subject can face the loss of the object, thanks to the constitution of a fantasy that consists in the imaginary representation of the lost object. In this sense, what guides sublimation concerns the dimension of loss and lack, as Freud and Lacan emphasize. The archaic and regressive quality of the quest orients the unconscious of the subject, impulsing the creation of the objects of sublimation. This archaic quality would account for the 'raw' relation (Penot, 2001) that the subject maintains with the *Thing*. Thus, *Das Ding* appears as the cause of the most extraordinary creations of humanity, as 'the *causa* of the most fundamental human passion' (Lacan, 1986, p. 116). In *On private madness*, Green (1996) points out that the object of passion is unique and irreplaceable despite it being displaced and having a metaphorical quality. It is unique to the extent that it is related to the lost object, *Das Ding*. However, the latter can never be found and it is in this difference between wishing and waiting to find the object that the quest is situated and marked by tension. All the forms that have been created in relation to the *Thing* belong to the sphere of sublimation. In *L'éthique de la psychanalyse*, Lacan precises that sublimation 'elevates an object ... to the dignity of the *Thing*' (Lacan, 1986, p. 133, my own translation). What marks sublimation is the irreducible character of the subject's quest of the object, which goes back to the time of *Das Ding*. However, whatever form sublimation takes in literary, plastic, intellectual or other types of activity, the search has to go through the signifiers, that is language. We would add the idea that this search leans equally on the sensual and affective traces that are left in the body by the prehistoric object. In this sense, the quest, situated in the zone between semiotics (Kristeva, 1974) and language, creates a gap between the hallucinated satisfaction and the pursued one. The process of creation and invention of the object is never peaceful and is always tinted with a degree of suffering. This is the reason why the search goes beyond the pleasure principle but it is not exempt from *jouissance*. It would be useful to be reminded that there is opposition between pleasure and *jouissance*. The first can be grasped according to the pleasure principle that aims at the reduction of the tension, whereas the second keeps the tension inherent in desire and goes beyond the pleasure principle.

Object *a* and the transitional object

Lacan (1986) establishes a similarity between his concept of object *a* and Winnicott's concept of the *transitional object* (1958, 1971). The latter takes the place of the breast or the object of the first relation but it is not an internal object as it would be for Melanie Klein. Winnicott (1971) explains that it is not the object that is transitional but the function that it assures. Hence, the object represents the transition of the young child from the state of union with the mother to the state of differentiation, which results in the possibility of perceiving the object as external and separated. The intermediate zone of experience is not questioned and the adult does not interrogate the child in order to know whether the object belongs to the internal reality or the external (shared) reality. The tension arising from the necessity of the acceptance of reality is the most challenging and never-ending task of a human being. There would be no possibility of liberating oneself from the tension provoked by the acceptance of external reality if it were not for the existence of a *zone of illusion*. The latter is decisive in the constitution of the child's authentic self and continues to exist in adult life, thanks to art, religion, imaginative life and creative scientific work. In this sense, Lacan's conception of object *a*, which is situated in the orbit of the quest of the object, therefore in the orbit of illusion, assures a similar function for cultural objects, which are derived from transitional objects. If for Winnicott the acceptance of the reality principle depends on the possibility of situating oneself in a zone of intermediate experience, for Lacan its equivalent would be a zone in which the individual wishes for and waits to find the object. Winnicott's paradox 'to find–to create' the object would also be very meaningful for Lacan. If finding the object refers to the original object that can never be found, then it has to be created by means of symbolization and sublimation.

In his seminar *L'angoisse*, Lacan (1962–1963), confers a different signification to the concept of *transitional object*, in articulation with his notion of *transferable objects*. The infant's anxiety arising at the moment of weaning can be grasped if this process is visualized not only in terms of the loss of the breast that has satisfied the need, but also in terms of having renounced an object that has been experienced as part of the self. Winnicott (1971) and Tustin (1972) would coincide with Lacan with regard to the infant's illusion with respect to the breast as being part of the self, an illusion that creates a sense of narcissistic continuity. Hence for Lacan, the crucial moment of renouncing the breast leads to the apparition of *transferable objects* as equivalents of natural objects that represent the maternal body, such as the breast, the faeces, the phallus, the voice and the gaze. Later, the mirror stage confers an imaginary sense of wholeness to the body, restituting what has been lost during weaning. The substitution of natural objects by the transferable objects inaugurates the process of the psychic constitution. After having been detached from the maternal body, the five forms of object *a*, such as the breast, the faeces, the phallus, the voice and the gaze, are transferred to external objects. Hence, the latter become equivalents of the objects detached from the maternal body, as the analysis of little Dick illustrates.

In 'The importance of symbol–formation in the development of the ego', Klein (1930) discusses the analytic treatment of Dick, a four-year-old boy. In his seminar *Les écrits techniques*, Lacan (1953–1954) discusses the clinical genius of Klein, who had succeeded in leading Dick from the impossibility of relating to the objects in his surrounding environment, to the possibility of establishing equivalences between the objects that he imagined inside the maternal body and the external ones. This process had opened the way to symbol–formation. Thanks to the possibility of establishing imaginary equations between the objects fantasized inside the maternal body and the external objects, the human being is capable of deploying an almost infinite number of objects that can be used symbolically. Here, Lacan conceives symbol–formation as a process related to sublimation (Porge, 2018, p. 59).

We would say that Winnicott precisely situates the transitional object and transitional phenomena in the space between the objects fantasized inside the maternal body and the external objects. In this sense, the transitional object symbolizes the breast or another part-object. However, what is essential is not its symbolic value but its *use*, which leads to the recognition of the object outside one's sense of omnipotence. In 'The use of the object and relating through identifications', Winnicott (1971) establishes a sequence beginning with object-relating and ending in the use of the object. In object-relating the individual is isolated and invests in an object that does not have an independent existence, in opposition to the use of the object, which is part of a shared reality and is not the product of one's projections. Between these two points, notes Winnicott, lies the hardest trial in terms of human development. The individual has to give a place to the object out of the realm of his or her omnipotent control. The recognition that the object is not part of one's own projections and that it has an independent existence is achieved through unconscious destruction (Abram, 2007). If the object can survive the individual's destructivity, then the individual can use the object and love it. Winnicott underlines that the object is destroyed not only because it is out of the realm of the individual's omnipotent control but also because the destructivity aimed at the object places it necessarily outside his or

her omnipotence. The possibility for the individual to begin to live crea-
tively in the world of objects and sublimate is conditioned by the object's
survival to his or her destructivity.

Symbol-formation and sublimation in Melanie Klein

While Winnicott confers a central place to the mother's survival with
respect to the child's destructivity, Melanie Klein approaches it without
taking into consideration the environment's role. The child's aggressive
and sadistic fantasies directed against the maternal body become the
motive for reparation, which establishes the basis for the realization of sublimations (Segal, 1955). The fear of losing the object that has been attacked
in the fantasies and the resulting guilt feelings lie at the source of reparation. However, Lacan considers that the imaginary solution found by the
child to the aggressive fantasies would correspond partly to sublimation.
In this sense, Freud, Lacan and Laplanche would agree that the source of
authentic sublimations would not lie in guilt feelings, hence in the need
for reparation, but in the urge for curiosity and research. However, it will
be the study of the depressive position that will transform Klein's conception of sublimation. In 'A contribution to the psychogenesis of manic-
depressive states' (1935), she relates reparation to the depressive position and
remarks that the effort to repair and restore the loved object that has been
crushed is decisive in the process of sublimation. In his presentation to
the Spanish edition of *New directions in psychoanalysis*, Emilio Rodrigue
(1965) refers to Hanna Segal, who affirms that Melanie Klein had become
Kleinian thanks to her work 'A contribution to the psychogenesis of manic-
depressive states' (1935). By means of the concept of the depressive position, Klein had introduced a series of propositions that could be sys-
tematized into a theoretical corpus. In 'A psycho-analytical approach to
aesthetics', one of the papers that figure in *New directions in psycho-analysis*,
Segal (1955) points to the pivotal role of the depressive position in the
process of growth. At this stage, the child still feels under the pressure
of voracious and sadistic drives directed against the object. In the fantasies, the loved object is continuously attacked, crushed and destroyed. The
child's destructivity leads to the desire to restore and recreate the loved
object. However, the intense feelings of loss and guilt can give way to
reparation and restoration only if the depressive anxiety resulting from
the sadistic attacks can be tolerated by the ego. In cases where depressive
anxiety exceeds the limits of what the ego can tolerate, regression to the
schizoid–paranoid position occurs. Here, lies a critical point of passage
from the feelings of hostility and persecution inherent in the schizoid–
paranoid position to the sense of responsibility entailed by the recognition of one's aggressivity with respect to the object, which exists out of
the realm of one's omnipotence. In this sense, the critical passage from
the schizoid–paranoid position to the depressive position coincides with

Winnicott's (1971) point of view with respect to what he considers as the hardest trial of human development. The subject has to acknowledge that the object is not part of one's own projections and that it has an independent existence, acknowledgement that depends on the possibility of having reached the depressive position.

References

Abram, J. (2007). *The language of Winnicott*. London: Karnac.

Freud, S. (1950[1895]). *Project for a scientific psychology. SE*, 1: 295–387.

Freud, S. (1925h). Negation. *SE*, *19*: 235–239.

Green, A. (1996). *On private madness*. London: Routledge.

Klein, M. (1930). The importance of symbol-formation in the development of the ego. *International journal of psychoanalysis*, *11*, 24–39.

Klein, M. (1932). *The psycho-analysis of children*. London: Hogarth.

Klein, M. (1935). A contribution to the psychogenesis of manic-depressive states. *International Journal of Psychoanalysis*, *16*, 145–174.

Kristeva, J. (1974). *La révolution du langage poétique*. Paris: Seuil.

Lacan, J. (1953–1954). *Le séminaire. Livre I. Les écrits techniques de Freud*. Paris: Seuil, 1975.

Lacan, J. (1962–1963). *Le séminaire. Livre X. L'angoisse*. Paris: Seuil, 2004.

Lacan, J. (1986). *Le séminaire. Livre VII. L'éthique de la Psychanalyse*. Paris: Seuil.

Masson, J.M. (Ed.) (1985). Letter 52. December 6. In: *The complete letters of Sigmund Freud to Wilhelm Fliess, 1887–1904*. Boston, MA: Harvard University Press.

Penot, P. (2001). *La passion du sujet freudien*. Paris: Erès.

Porge, E. (2018). *La sublimation, une érotique pour la psychanalyse*. Paris: Erès.

Rodrigué, E. (1965). Presentacion de la edicion castellana. In: M. Klein, P. Heimann & R.E. Money-Kyrle (Eds.), *Nuevas direcciones en psicoanalisis*. Buenos Aires: Paidos.

Segal, H. (1955). A psycho-analytical approach to aesthetics. In: M. Klein, P. Heimann & R.E. Money-Kyrle (Eds.), *New directions in psychoanalysis*. London: Tavistock Press.

Tustin, F. (1972). *Autism and childhood psychosis*. London: Hogarth.

Winnicott, D.W. (1958). Transitional objects and transitional phenomena. *Collected Papers: Through Pediatrics to Psycho-Analysis*. London: Tavistock Publications.

Winnicott, D.W. (1971). Use of an object and relating through identifications. *Playing and reality*. London: Tavistock Publications.

11 Psychoanalytic writing and the unknown

Femininity and the thinking quality of the woman analyst

Years ago I discovered in an art gallery in San Juan (Puerto Rico) the work of Myrna Baez, a famous woman painter and printmaker, which impressed me; it figured a naked woman sitting by a window that was open onto nature. The woman's meditative position evoked that of Rodin's *The thinker*. Her nakedness was disturbing and supported the act of thinking, as her meditative position indicated it. The window opening onto nature represented the frontier between the inside and outside as well as the passage from one to the other. The woman was represented as a thinker but also embodied feminine qualities, evoked by her nakedness. The woman here, both in her femininity and thinking quality, seems like a representation of a woman psychoanalyst who is absorbed in the passion of elaborating and theorizing with respect to her psychoanalytic work. In his seminar *L'éthique de la psychanalyse*, Lacan (1986) names the elaboration and deepening of analytic thought as ethics, and remarks that sublimation should also be considered in terms of ethics. The desire of the analyst lies in the heart of the urge to elaborate and deepen analytic knowledge and thought. Lacan underlines the place that Freud had accorded to sublimation. 'Sublimation is in fact the other face of the exploration that Freud makes as a pioneer, of the roots of the ethical feeling' (Lacan, 1986, p. 105, my own translation). Erik Porge (2018) addresses the question of sublimation specific to the analyst, which concerns the way he or she works and practices analysis in relation to signifiers such as desire, love and *jouissance*. This is the reason why sublimation would be a kind of ethics of the erotic and he designates it by a neologism produced by the combination of the two terms: it is an *erothics* (*érothique*) (Porge, 2018, p. 8). In this sense, Porge agrees with Lacan's point of view.

The desire of the analyst

In his seminar *L'éthique de la psychanalyse*, Lacan (1986) points to the existence of a turning point at the end of analysis. If the analysand can accept the sole responsibility of his or her destiny and can appropriate it, then

DOI: 10.4324/9781003232261-11

there is a shift from the position of analysand to that of analyst, under-lain by the function of the 'desire of the analyst'. We know that Lacan places the desire of the analyst in the heart of the psychoanalytic experience and this is what confers its ethical dimension to it. The analyst's desire implies the possibility of authorizing himself or herself to be an analyst and situate as such. The psychoanalytic institution's acknowl-edgement of the analyst with respect to the exercise of analysis is not sufficient, as indicated by the difficulties that the candidates and even analysts have in authorizing themselves for such work. The analysand's confrontation with his or her destiny at the end of analysis does not consist in a sacrifice or a renunciation. On the contrary, it means that the analysand can assume the losses and the suffering inherent in his or her own life, without reproaching or accusing others, particularly the parents. This is the moment when the analysand becomes a desiring subject. Here, lies the decisive place of the constitution of the Lacanian subject as well as that of the passage from the position of analysand to that of the analyst. The constitution of the subject has as a condition the capacity to invert his or her own lack, that which opens access to desire. The lack ensuing from the need provokes an unending demand that can never be compensated and satisfied. A gap continues to exist between the need and the demand. In this sense, desire is tragic as it does not aim at reducing the lack or rendering it tolerable. On the contrary, it means that the subject is ready to pay the price for 'desiring the desire' and it is always via the transgression of his or her limits, a beneficial trans-gression, that the subject can experience it. However, renouncing one's own desire means obeying the exigencies of the super-ego and this solu-tion is much more comfortable than assuming the risks and uncertainty underlying the assumption of one's desire. At this point Lacan points out a paradox: the more the individual gives up his or her own wishes, the more the super-ego becomes cruel and implacable. Traditional ethics would consist in reducing the success of an analysis to a comfortable position related to the acquisition of goods, goods of the family, goods of the house, goods of the profession and so on, which are evidently reasonable. However, Lacan opposes traditional ethics in favour of psy-choanalytic ethics. In this sense, there is an opposition between the material acquisition of goods and the *good* resulting from the realization of one's desire; the acquisition of goods 'does not necessarily resolve the question of the actual relation of each man, in this short space between his birth and his death, with respect to his own desire' (Lacan, 1986, p. 351, my own translation). At the term of an analysis, the process that prepares the analysand to become an analyst corresponds to the con-frontation with the reality of the human condition. This point of solitude is tragic, as the analysand can no more blame anyone for what has been than for what has not been, and this requires the mourning of what has not been realized.

After having completed their long training process, analysts find themselves in a daily routine. However, it is the desire to learn and pursue the unknown about their patients and themselves that can precisely transform this routine. Michel de M'Uzan (2005) remarks that analysts should reflect about themselves: Am I working as an analyst, do I continue to be an analyst? To be able to work and stay as an analyst depends on the capacity to elaborate the resistances that impede any kind of change with respect to one's identity. However, this change requires a continuous process of learning and transformation. Patrick Guyomard (1998) concurs with de M'Uzan and notes that the assumption of the patient's transference by the analyst consists in becoming responsible for the work that is realized as well as in accounting for the unconscious. Here, the decisive point does not involve only acting like a real analyst but being able to *stay as such*. It is 'the desire of the analyst' that confers an identity to the work realized and this is an aspect that has been emphasized by Lacan. The analyst's relation to the desire-of-the-analyst as a function concerns the assumption of his or her castration, that which originates desire. In this sense, analytic function consists in a particular way of relating not only to psychoanalytic knowledge but also to the unknown and this precisely becomes the motive for writing.

Why do analysts write?

In 1977, in a special number of *Nouvelle revue de psychanalyse* dedicated to writing psychoanalysis, an exchange takes place between Michel de M'Uzan and Jean-Bertrand Pontalis. Writing gives the analyst the opportunity to return to the work with patients and reflect on it. Hence, the transference and counter-transference processes that lie at the heart of the analytic experience become the reason why analysts write. De M'Uzan wishes to know how the analysts, who are on 'permission' from their counter-transference during their summer vacations, spend their time. Analysts write during their vacations and they write precisely on psychoanalysis and this is a paradox. While the analysts need to have a pause with respect to the work with their patients, writing consists in returning to the same work in another way. One day, one of André Green's (1977) former analysands asked him the reason why he wrote. He answered that his writing was a means of offering a testimony but he had not told him that he could not exist without writing. This gives us an idea of the degree to which the desire to know and write can be passionate. The analyst is taken by the urge to give voice to something that makes him or her suffer and cannot do otherwise. Hence, writing becomes a way of thinking on analytic experience and it is through this mode of communication that the analysts expose themselves in a style that is characteristic of them. Writing is a testimony with respect to one's experience and involves a way of revealing oneself. Bion's style, according to Green, consists in the painful sensitiveness of a person that has been skinned. In the first tome of his memoirs, *A long week-end* (1982), Bion refers to the sense of devastation that he had experienced as a young officer, when he had not been able to protect his soldiers and avoid their death. This traumatic experience had haunted him for many years.

Theorizing becomes an attempt to overcome the unknown inherent in the psyche. Evidently, the art of the analyst nowadays corresponds to the necessity to grasp not only the unconscious processes that can be represented but also those that have no representation and cannot be symbolized. These processes concern in the first place the analyst, who is taken by the urge to know and understand both the patient and himself or herself. In this sense, the psyche is *par excellence* the object of knowledge. Referring to Bion, Simone Korff-Sausse (2010) remarks that the psyche is not only the object of knowledge but also the instrument of knowledge. The question that the analyst faces is how to comprehend the analytic experience and transmit it? Bion was particularly concerned, notes Korff-Sausse, by the transmission of the analytic experience and by the search of an adequate mode of communication that could account for it. He considered that verbal language was not sufficient for it to the extent that psychic experience originates in sensory experiences. This leads to the necessity to find–create an adequate style of writing that can reflect the patient's tempestuous affects belonging to the early phases of childhood but also to those that arise in the analytic space between the analyst and the analysand. What draws our attention is Korff-Sausse's conception with respect to psychoanalytic writing as an original writing, whose aim is neither artistic nor purely scientific. It is in the act of writing that the analyst creates something that belongs to the sphere of the unnameable, the invisible and the formless.

During the analytic process, the analyst's sensitiveness and acceptance of a temporary loss of his or her sense of identity become the way to grasp the unknown. In *A beam of intense darkness* (2007), James Grotstein writes on Bion, who has been his analyst but also his master. He precises that the Bionian unconscious differs from the Freudian and the Kleinian conceptions of the unconscious. Bion's universe is three-legged, composed of psychic reality, external reality and the unknown, the latter being situated in the intersection between the two realities. In this sense, the analyst's endeavour to grasp the analytic process is situated in the zone of the unknown, which is the cause of investigation and writing. Along with the resolution of the conflicts with respect to the primitive affects, such as envy, greed, hate and omnipotence, an analysis should permit the patient to access the 'negative capability' as well as the depressive position. Hence, the appropriation of one's history takes place in a permanent quest for oneself. By emphasizing Bion's mystic aspect, Grotstein appeals to the mystic part of each of us. Mystics accept their personal destiny and the negative capability acquires its full meaning here.

However, this position does not signify that the subject has to resign to his or her destiny and accept it passively and blindly. On the contrary, it requires the courage and passion to travel through the unknown of life, in the effort to invert one's destiny. In a surprising way, Bion's idea coincides with Lacan's point of view. In fact, Bion had been influenced not only by Freud and Melanie Klein but also by Lacan. The deciphering of the unconscious forces that configure the analytic space as well as the symbolization of contents that have no representation constitute the place from which we write. The effort to grasp and elaborate these forces corresponds to sublimation. On the other hand, the analyst's competence ensuing from a rich theoretical knowledge and clinical experience would not be sufficient if it were not nourished by the cultural world. In fact, analytic experience has to be nourished by the milk of culture. The relation with cultural objects, such as plastic arts, visual arts, literature, music, journeys to different cultures and so on, allows the analyst to speak in the language of dreams. Freud (1930a) notes that once the neurotic patient's inhibitions are overcome, sublimation can silently and by itself find an expression both inside and outside analysis. The patient is taken by the wish to explore and deepen his or her discoveries with respect to psychical reality and experiences a satisfaction by its realization. Hence, sublimation in analysis is related to the patient's wish and curiosity to explore the unknown and symbolize the contents relative to it. Bion (1970) defines this curiosity as the quest for the truth, whereas Grotstein (2007)names it in a more radical way as the 'truth drive'. However, the scope of what the analysand can discover about himself or herself depends on the analyst's relation with the unknown and the degree to which the analyst can extend the journey through the unknown. The analyst's relation with the unknown depends on what Guyomard (1998) defines as the desire-of-the-analyst as a function. This is why psychoanalytic experience is not relative to knowledge that refers to contents that can be defined and are accessible within certain limits, but concerns desire, the desire to know, which always confronts the subject with a transgression. Piera Aulagnier (1986) remarks that the desire to know has always been the object of prohibition, representing the extreme limit that the human being should never transgress. The transgression of the prohibition to know and its consequences have been illustrated by myths and in particular by the myth of Oedipus.

At the termination of an analysis, the quest to know and the desire to extend it through the unknown can convert an analysand into an analyst. The subject is from then on in the position of a desiring subject and in search of the unknown, thanks to a continuous transgression of the known. In this sense, the desire to know as a passionate quest is infinite. Kristeva (2005) underlines the serenity created by thinking, speaking, knowing and writing. In her memoirs, *The force of circumstance*, Simone de Beauvoir (1966) confesses that the writing of *The second sex* (2014) had allowed her to express herself in all serenity. Virginia Woolf describes a similar process. In *A writer's diary*, she notes that 'it is a serene, accomplished feeling, to write' (Woolf, 1981 p. 122). We know, however, that to be able to attain this quality implies having undergone a long journey inside oneself as well as in the world and requires courage, particularly when it is question of a woman.

References

Aulagnier, P. (1986). Le 'désir de savoir' dans ses rapports à la trangression. *Un interprète en quête de sens*. Paris: Ramsay.

Barthes, R. (1973). *Le plaisir du texte*. Paris: Seuil.

Barthes, R. (1975). *The pleasure of the text*. New York: Hill & Wang.

De Beauvoir, S. (1949). *Le deuxième sexe II*. Paris: Gallimard.

De Beauvoir, S. (1963). *La force des choses I*. Paris: Gallimard.

De Beauvoir, S. (1963). *La force des choses II*. Paris: Gallimard.

De Beauvoir, S. (1966). *The force of circumstance*. London: Weidenfeld & Nicolson.

De Beauvoir, S. (2014). *The second sex*. London: Vintage.

De M'Uzan, M. (2005). *Aux confins de l'identité*. Paris: Gallimard.

De M'Uzan, M. & Pontalis, J.-B. (1977). Ecrire, psychanalyser, écrire. *Nouvelle revue de psychanalyse*, 16, 5–26.

Bion, W.R. (1970). *Attention and interpretation*. London: Tavistock.

Bion, W. (1982). *The long week-end. 1897–1919*. London: Routledge.

Freud, S. (1930a). *Civilization and its discontents*. *SE*, 21: 64–145.

Green, A. (1977). Transcription d'origine inconnue. *Nouvelle revue de psychanalyse*, 16, 27–63.

Grotstein J.S. (2007). *A beam of intense darkness*. London: Karnac.

Guyomard, P. (1998). *La jouissance du tragique*. Paris: Gallimard.

Korff-Sausse, S. (2010). Le psychanalyste 'écrivant'. Ecrire la psychanalyse avec W.R. Bion. *Revue française de psychanalyse*, 74:2, 389–400.

Kristeva, J. (2005). Le langage, la sublimation, les femmes. *La haine et le pardon*. Paris: Fayard.

Lacan, J. (1986). *Le séminaire. Livre VII. L'éthique de la psychanalyse*. Paris: Seuil.

Porge, E. (2018). *La sublimation, une érotique pour la psychanalyse*. Paris: Erès.

Woolf, V. (1981). *A writer's diary*. New York: Harvest Publications.

Index

For Product Safety Concerns and Information please contact our EU
representative GPSR@taylorandfrancis.com
Taylor & Francis Verlag GmbH, Kaufingerstraße 24, 80331 München, Germany

www.ingramcontent.com/pod-product-compliance
Lightning Source LLC
Chambersburg PA
CBHW070348270326
41926CB00017B/4042